THE MYSTERY OF HEALING

by the

Theosophical Research Centre

A QUEST BOOK

*This publication made possible
with the assistance of the Kern Foundation*

THE THEOSOPHICAL PUBLISHING HOUSE

Wheaton, Ill., U.S.A.
Madras, India/London, England

First published 1958

First Quest Book revised edition 1968, published by The
Theosophical Publishing House, a department of The Theosophical Society in America, Wheaton, Illinois, by special
arrangement with The Theosophical Publishing House (London) Ltd.

Second Quest edition, 1977.

ISBN: 0-8356-0114-5

Printed in the United States of America

FOREWORD

THIS book is intended as a sequel to 'Some Unrecognized Factors in Medicine', first published in 1934 and again, in a revised edition, ten years later. It is the work of the same group of the Theosophical Research Centre in England, whose members are M. Beddow Bayly, M.R.C.S., L.R.C.P., Laurence J. Bendit, M.A., M.D., Mrs Phoebe D. Bendit, H. Tudor Edmunds, M.B., B.S., Mrs Adelaide Gardner, B.A. The latter did most of the compilation and the group would like to record their sincere thanks to her.

The purpose of this second book is to carry further the study of the principles outlined in the first, in the hope of clarifying to some extent the confusion which exists in many minds regarding unusual methods of healing. It is of little use to talk about spiritual healing unless one has some idea of what is denoted by the word spirit, as distinct from soul or psyche. The same applies to the term 'vital energy'. On such points the student of Theosophy and of the occult tradition can offer, if not scientific knowledge, at least suggestive ideas, with more clarity and definition than the Churches or the Spiritualists have so far achieved.

From a popular standpoint it would doubtless have been better to have written without reference to occult doctrines. But to do so would have been to restrict ourselves to precisely the same ambiguous concepts which are one of the main causes of confusion. It is important nowadays to be able to offer a reasoned explanation for the occurrence of miracles, as well as for their failure to occur—for intelligent people can only see a miracle as a fulfilment of law, not as an abrogation of it, an intensification of nature rather than something unnatural—and it is only from the viewpoint from which this book is written that such a thing can be done. This is not to say that everything is explained; that can never be, for if every mystery of nature were made plain, man would lose his particular prerogative, which is that of constant enquiry, and investigation of the world in which he lives.

It is in the exercise of that prerogative that this book was written. It is offered in the hope that, just as its predecessor has proved useful to students, this one may be equally helpful.

L. J. BENDIT

THE Eternal Providence has appointed me to watch over the life and health of Thy creatures. May the love of my art actuate me at all times; may neither avarice, nor miserliness, nor thirst for glory, or for great reputation engage my mind; for the enemies of truth and philanthropy could easily deceive me and make me forgetful of my lofty aim of doing good to Thy children. May I never see in the patient anything but a fellow creature in pain. Grant me strength, time and opportunity always to correct what I have acquired, always to extend its domain; for knowledge is immense and the spirit of man can extend infinitely to enrich itself daily with new requirements. To-day he can discover his errors of yesterday and to-morrow he may obtain a new light on that which he thinks himself sure of to-day. O God, Thou hast appointed me to watch over the life and death of Thy creatures; here am I ready for my vocation. And now I turn unto my calling.

THE OATH OF MAIMONIDES

CONTENTS

ACKNOWLEDGEMENTS

We wish to express thanks to Messrs Chatto & Windus;
Faber and Faber, Ltd; Charles Scribner's Sons; and the
Student Christian Movement Press, Ltd. for their kind
permission to print as chapter headings quotations from
books published by their respective firms.

CHAPTER I

INTRODUCTION

> The assumption that the mind is a real being, which can be acted upon by the brain, and which can act on the body through the brain, is the only one compatible with all the facts of experience.
>
> 'Elements of Physiological Psychology', *George T. Ladd*

FROM time immemorial man has been interested in problems of health and disease, but there are periods of history when special attention is focussed on the more mysterious and deeper aspects of the matter. These usually coincide with crises in human affairs when man is thrown back on himself and endeavours to find a solution to his difficulties from within rather than from without. At present we are in one of these periods, but with the difference that there exists, in direct contrast to the science of the inner man, the extraverted science of the day, which seeks to find the answer to every problem in terms of matter alone and of the energies which govern and create that matter.

We have thus in the field of medicine two schools of thought. One looks at man from within outwards and is allied to the teachings of such students as Paracelsus, Mesmer, Charcot and the early French psychologists, later followed by Freud, Jung, and others. The other group makes it their whole endeavour to explain all the phenomena of life, and hence those of health and disease, in terms of physical mechanisms, biochemistry and the like.

It must be admitted that those who have built machines out of units suggested by the reactions found in nerve-cells have succeeded surprisingly well in imitating animal behaviour, and even some of the functions of a brain. But it seems quite beyond the bounds of possibility that this method will ever produce a machine able to act consciously, or that is capable of self-reproduction or self-repair. Against this, and at the other extreme, there are the thousands of people who believe that they have the power to heal the sick by means which are anything but those of ordinary science or mechanics—and who, indeed, on rare occasions, seem to produce something akin to a miracle. These unorthodox healers, when successful, appear to give their patients something they need, which brings about an alleviation of their disease symptoms; yet such improvements are frequently temporary. The lame who suddenly walk, and throw away their crutches, often have to ask for new ones, and patients relieved of pain later find their root trouble untouched.*

Nevertheless there remains the fact that in a few cases some sort of cure does take place in both organic and functional disease through various unorthodox methods of treatment. There are also many instances of arrest and cure of disease conditions without any physical treatment having been given. What is the method by which such healing works? What laws govern its action? Can these laws be known, studied, and certain conditions determined in which the influences involved will act more easily?

It is the purpose of this book to try to restate certain age-old teachings that throw light upon such problems. The principles involved concern the relation of man to his body, and the interactions between human consciousness and physical matter which affect the processes of physical, psychological, psychic, and spiritual healing.

These ancient teachings, known always to a few serious students, have in the last century once more been made public and accessible to those who are prepared to study them carefully. They have gone under many names: here we shall call them the Perennial Philosophy, or the Ancient Wisdom. They were, and are, the heart of all Mystery School teaching throughout the ages, for these Schools were not merely religious and ethical, but theurgic— explaining the interplay of unseen but potent forces, and their action upon visible matter. The theories put forward explain not only the evolution of matter, but likewise that of consciousness, and give indications of many of the laws by which the little understood forces of the unseen worlds act deeply upon living tissues in all kingdoms. The field covered is so extensive that we shall take from it only those considerations which affect the problem of personal healing. For our purpose it will be useful to study how living tissues are influenced by unseen forces, some of which emanate from other kingdoms as well as from the human.

These teachings are not stated dogmatically, but should be taken as hypotheses only, to be tested by experiment and applica-

* See Chapter VII and Appendix B for further details.

tion. It is the opinion of the present writers that, used in this fashion, they give probably the most consistent, rational and illuminative explanation covering *all* the facts known about psychological and psychic healing, and point to possibilities of further investigation which are full of promise.

The principles involved are by no means easy to understand, for they demand that new values be given to the power of thought, of emotion, and of habit at all levels. They describe powers latent in every man, and active in the few. They even suggest the existence of conscious and intelligent entities other than human beings—invisible, and functioning in full consciousness in ways about which we know very little, but with certain activities that interact with human experience.

It is on the basis of these teachings, combined with those of modern science, that this book is founded. The writers feel that in the present muddled state of thought on this important subject, here is at least a coherent theory that will bear examination, and make sense of facts, evidence, and personal experience, which otherwise appear chaotic and irrational.

CHAPTER II

THE HEALING PROCESS IN GENERAL

In this sense we really can enjoy poor health; not as hysterics
do, with truth reversed and invalidism exploited for the power
that it can offer: but accepting it with joy, as something to be
suffered and passed through creatively.

'The Invisible Anatomy', *Graham Howe*

THE phrase 'the patient as a whole' occurs often in current
medical literature and may now be said to be widely accepted
as the guiding principle of treatment among the foremost practitioners of to-day. But from the point of view of the writers of this
book, the wholeness of man implies a fuller conception of his
constitution than that usually ascribed to the term.

The spiritual principle needs to be included as well as the
physical, emotional, and mental principles. Unfortunately, the
words 'spirit' and 'spiritual' are often employed rather loosely,
and without any very precise meaning. In this book spirit is
envisaged as the primary factor—the *fons et origo*—in human
consciousness; while the psyche—the mental-emotional factor, or
soul—is regarded as subsidiary to it. The physical body, important
as it undoubtedly is, represents but the visible, outer result of the
interaction of the spirit, and its instrument the soul, with the
physical world. In other words, the physical body is the indispensable medium through which the inner man gains experience
in, and acts upon, his physical environment. Thus, in using the
phrase 'the wholeness of man', the writers regard spirit as the all-
inclusive background of every aspect of the human being, the
physical body never being thought of as apart from the human
spirit but as a special manifestation of its activity.

Modern medicine has tended to concentrate so exclusively upon
the elaborations of physical detail, and has assembled such a vast
array of more or less important material concerning the physical
mechanism, that the real significance of the inner man, the
consciousness that uses the body, has often failed to be recognized.
Psychological medicine, which has received so much greater
recognition in recent years than hitherto, constitutes a healthy

and inevitable reaction to the treatment of patients on a purely material basis. Yet even to-day, the phrase 'treating the whole man', which has come into more frequent use, implies in many schools of thought only slight acknowledgement of the existence of the psyche and of its relation to health.

There are still far too few who realize that healing is primarily a spiritual process proceeding from within outwards, from the spiritual centre to the circumference of the physical body. Thus the role of therapy in any of its various forms is not so much an active as a permissive one, and consists very largely in providing the pre-requisite conditions at all levels through which the healing process can assert itself.

Professor Maxwell Telling once remarked: 'Good medicine consists in rest, nursing, diet; and the use of drugs is to assist and palliate when required.' We would agree with this as far as it goes, but the statement is far from complete, and we shall be more concerned with discussing the fundamental *causes* of disease and their removal, rather than with the superficial manifestations of disease and methods appropriate to their palliation. Superficial symptoms may often be suppressed with apparently brilliant results, only to find later that a fresh complication has arisen, because the real cause has not been touched, while in some cases the treatment itself has resulted in 'side effects'.

The modern emphasis on preventive aspects of medicine in such matters as diet, hygiene, environment and working conditions is admirable as far as it goes. But it is still far too much engrossed with seeking immunity from specific diseases by means of short-cuts, such as the use of prophylactic inoculations, and too little with probing the fundamental causes and applying commonsense methods which promote what is already being described as 'positive health'.

Dr H. P. Newsholme summed up this view admirably in 'Health, Disease and Integration'. He wrote: 'Medicine is only on the verge of its real sphere of activity, on which it will enter when it can systematically treat the individual as an intimate moulding, not merely of body and mind in their delicate adjustment to each other, but of the body and mind as the vessel for the reception and expression of the spirit'.

Bearing these preliminary observations in mind, we should now be in a better position to formulate what we really mean by the terms health and healing. *Normal health may be said to be present when a person is at peace with himself and is in a harmonious relationship with his whole environment.* This relationship is essentially a vital and not a static one, and involves an interlacing of outgoing and incoming forces at each level of consciousness and in each field of activity. It can never be considered as precisely determined, but as in constant movement and re-adjustment. When the flow both outwards and inwards is normal—normal, that is, for the particular individual concerned at any given time— the tendency is for him to feel both well and happy; in other words, he is for the time being well adjusted to the immediate circumstances whatever they may be.*

Happiness in this sense is neither simple contentment nor intense excitement, but consists in a harmonious or 'right' relationship to life and experience at any given time. As such, it is a basic condition in nature—one towards which the forces of nature tend. But it is never fixed or static, being, as stated, a constant flow of successive adjustments that result in growth; that is, in the assimilation of ever-expanding experience.

From this point of view, pain, ill-health and unhappiness are all seen to be the result of maladjustment at different levels of experience. In other words, they indicate a lack of free harmonious interaction between an area or organ of the body and its associated activities, or between the individual and his environment, including, of course, his fellow beings.

From this it naturally follows that the process of healing, whatever may be the particular method employed or the field of activity involved, should be regarded fundamentally as the restoration of the normal relationships already mentioned. During a long illness the period of time involved may be necessary in order to allow for the making of some deep-seated readjustment to what is probably a relatively new and unaccustomed situation; on the other hand, not more than a few hours' rest may be sufficient to ensure recovery from some slight shock or injury.

Healing may appear to be spontaneous, or accidental, or to take place as the result of the administration of this or that medicine or treatment; but, basically, in all cases where it is really successful, it is due to the achievement, or restoration, of the

---

* See 'Some Unrecognized Factors in Medicine', Conclusion. Theosophical Publishing House, London.

correct relationship between the diseased area and the body; between the body and its environment; and above all between the individual, his body, and his personal relationships. Hence, rest, change of environment, or a complete alteration in mental attitude, will often bring about a re-adjustment in relationships that results in a spontaneous cure. Slight accidents, such as a fall, or a shock as trivial as a sneeze, have been known to initiate a healing process, presumably through the adjustment of tensions effected by that shock.

One hears much about miraculous cures, but it needs to be emphasized that neither medicines nor any other purely physical types of treatment can bring these about, although, given the right conditions of time, place, mood, and circumstance, the healing that follows their application may be remarkably swift and complete. The explanation lies in the fact that, whatever the method, healing takes place as soon as the patient becomes reasonably well reintegrated and life again flows more or less easily and normally between himself and his surroundings.

Here it may be well to introduce the idea, no doubt startling to some readers, that death of the physical body may be the occasion and sign of a true healing. It is a release from hitherto limiting and frustrating conditions which have now become no longer necessary because the inner conflict or maladjustment of which they were the symptom has been resolved. The patient is therefore enabled to continue his progress in the next sphere of human existence, untrammelled by the limitations he has now outgrown.

As a natural corollary, it would appear that even a protracted and painful illness may supply the much-needed opportunity for readjustment to take place at interior levels. But once the inner disturbance has been resolved, either physical recovery or the dissolution of the body follows, and may be welcomed as an indication that the lesson has, at any rate for the time being, been assimilated.

The 'river of healing' is always present in the world. Like life itself, it defies definition, but it is an active force manifesting at all levels of existence. It can be touched in many ways, often unexpectedly. As often as not it is passed by unseen, or unrecognized, for it is usually the conditions within the patient himself which obscure its presence and obstruct its beneficent flow.

CHAPTER III

SOME FACTORS IN HEALTH AND DISEASE

The great thing in all spiritual healing is the arousing of the
faith of the patient to the point at which healing forces, physical
and mental, can dominate the organism. ... This may need
different methods for each patient. Each can only acquire it in
his own way.
                    'Religion and Psychology', *A. Graham Ikin*

Life's greatest solace to a soul in distress is the understanding
and sympathy of a friend.   *Anon*

There is not a single problem, however sinister, which the
power of friendship cannot resolve.   *G. S. Arundale*

CHANGING VIEWS

IN periods of rapid transition such as the present, there are not
only marked changes in current modes of thinking, but life
itself becomes more full of stresses than in times that are regarded
as normal. In the field of medicine, these conditions are reflected
in changing views on the nature of health and of disease, and
even of man himself, as well as in the increase of mental and
emotional stresses suffered by patients. There is apt to be a time-
lag however between the occurrence of special strains which beset
individuals in a changing world, and the realization that it is these
strains which are the cause of seemingly new types of organic
disturbance. In short, the current view of the nature of man, and
so of the background of disease conditions, lags behind the
knowledge of disease itself and of its bacteriological factors.

Thus to-day a materialistic outlook in medicine, as in other
branches of biology, is trying to keep pace with new ideas concerning human nature, and with new concepts of psychological
conflict in which the physical body plays only a secondary role.
Nevertheless the background to medical philosophy is changing
rapidly, and many views that were held as sacrosanct a few de-
cades ago are being challenged, if not as yet discarded. The
microbic theory of disease is an example. Microbes exist in
myriads, yet only about one per cent are nowadays thought to be

in themselves noxious, and then only when the body is in such a state as to provide a suitable 'soil'. It is also well known that without the friendly hosts of bacteria which inhabit it, the animal organism could not survive. This is a very far cry from Pasteur. Similarly, the principles behind the modern view of psychosomatic medicine are daily gaining greater acceptance, while the field assigned to psychosomatic diseases is constantly widened.*

THE PATIENT AS A WHOLE

One of the most marked changes in medical outlook since the last war has been in the attitude towards the patient. At one time the main aim of the physician may be said to have been that of trying to find a focus of infection. Later the tendency was to concentrate attention upon a particular tissue or organ, perhaps in terms of biochemistry—all leading to a tendency to specialize in treatment of one aspect or another of the organism. But to-day medical literature constantly refers to 'the patient as a whole', and disease is looked upon as something different from its local manifestation, whether in cell growth or in localized metabolic disturbance.†

It is also realized that, although the individual patient is of primary importance, in order to see him in a proper light he has to be thought of as existing in relationship with others. Man is social in his fundamental nature and lives in a community of which he is an integral part. In recognition of this fact, the doctor in many countries is now expected to consider the patient in relation to his integration with his home, his work, and his obligations as a citizen. The doctor himself has become a social servant equipped with special if inadequate opportunities for recommending psychological treatment as well as for dealing with physical difficulties. While this tendency has not, on the part of orthodox medicine, gone much beyond the recognition of the significance of the psyche, or soul—the spirit being still ignored, certain very well known psychologists and distinguished medical men include the spiritual nature as an essential factor in their consideration of the patient under treatment.

* See 'Trends in Modern Medicine', by M. Beddow Bayly, M.R.C.S., L.R.C.P.
† See 'British Medical Association Report on Medical Education', *British Medical Journal*, September 7, 1957: 'A Prescription for Health', R. W. Luxton, F.R.C.P.

SOCIAL MEDICINE

Thus the social aspects of disease are beginning to be dealt with, and preventive medicine is gaining ground, but it must be admitted that while some of the methods used seem to tend to real improvement in health, the ultimate results of others are dubious. The ideal of such treatments is to forestall the onset of disease whenever possible, rather than to wait until it is established before bringing it under treatment, but the view of the cause of disease is still far too materialistic. As we have noted, even psychologists and psychiatrists fail to recognize the most creative element in man, the innermost spirit. Serious concern has been expressed of late by many eminent medical people over the fact that although vast sums of money are now being spent upon preventive measures—diet, vaccinations, inoculations and health-education propaganda—there is ever increasing evidence of the growth of subtle nervous disorders, as well as of psychological difficulties, which are very difficult to cure.

In considering this increase in nervous disorders, one may hold the pressure, speed, noise, and other stresses of modern life largely responsible. But the widespread use of vaccinations against this and that disease, which upset chemical balance and the biological integrity of the tissues, must be regarded as equally culpable, and as having deleterious results which may last a lifetime in certain individuals. At the other end of the scale, there is a lack of spiritual incentive in life which is increasingly evident, and which is nowadays admitted to have a fundamental influence upon personal health and well being.*

From the facts mentioned above, it is clear that the old view of infective disease is giving place to greater emphasis upon the field in which the microbe develops, rather than upon the presence of the microbe in this or that tissue. This field is the individual himself, and it is to changes within that individual that the diagnostician must look if he would find the basic reason for the development of a dangerous infection. The patient may become open to the undesirable development of an infective micro-organism for many reasons. There may be a metabolic disorder, due to faulty feeding; or some psychic or mental shock may lead

* See 'Disease and the Social System' by Arthur Guirdham, Chapters VIII and XII. Allen and Unwin.

to unstable metabolism; or tissues may be damaged by physical injury. True, a given microbe determines the exact nature of the illness, but only after it has found a fertile field in a system that has hitherto been immune to it.

MODERN METHODS: USEFUL AND DUBIOUS

Working on purely hygienic and bacteriological lines, preventive medicine has made great strides in certain directions, so that some of the scourges of fifty years ago, such as scarlet fever or typhoid, are nowadays very little feared, especially in countries that have improved nutrition and developed effective care for social hygiene. Also certain new drugs have been found which, at least as far as immediate results go, give spectacular results, both in the prevention and in the cure of many diseases.

But among these drugs are the vaccines, and kindred preparations. Serious doubts arise as to the validity of this form of preventive medicine. Inoculations may immunize children against diseases, which, serious as they may be when they afflict a single patient, are statistically only likely to attack a small percentage of those exposed to them. Such inoculations are not harmless since they all cause protein shock and can give rise to grave reactions, such as anaphylaxis, or in some instances to a serious form of the disease itself. One is entitled to ask whether if one could measure the overall benefit to the community, the ill-effects of such widespread practices, subtle and insidious as they are, may not in the aggregate be worse than the fact that one individual here or there may suffer from a direct infection.

In the field of hygiene and dietetics there is also a growing doubt about certain modern usages. In general, there is wider appreciation of the value of fresh foods and of the relative nutritional value of various edibles. But while food on the whole is handled more cleanly than it used to be, and hence gastrointestinal diseases are fewer, its quality has suffered. Dishonest commercialism makes use of supposedly harmless cheap dyes to suggest the presence of important ingredients that are in fact absent; preservatives are used to embalm foods which would otherwise perish and which are then sold as if they were fresh; refrigeration diminishes vitaminic content; refinement removes valuable parts of natural grain; hens are forced to lay in highly abnormal and unhealthy conditions in 'batteries'; cows are over-milked; and vegetables are grown more for size and market value than for their intrinsic nutriment, and often in soil which may be fertilized with artificial substitutes for the natural sources of plant food. So the benefits gained by hygiene may well be more than outweighed by denaturing practices applied to food supplies.

INCREASE OF MENTAL DISORDERS

Further, in spite of the efforts made to improve public health, there is the fact mentioned above that many more cases of mental breakdown, and of physical disease directly connected with mental overstrain, are occurring than ever before. The pace of life has quickened in every way, physically and intellectually, and the whole organism of man is subjected to stresses to which it is unaccustomed and to which many individuals are as yet unable to adapt themselves. Preventive mental hygiene, which should run parallel with physical measures, still lags far behind the need.

Amongst other factors leading to tension and collapse, consideration needs to be given not only to noise in general, but to the kind of noise which nowadays passes for popular music, and from which it is often impossible to escape in any public place. Some of this is innocuous enough, but some is definitely calculated to rouse the primitive in man, an aspect of himself which the more mature side of the individual normally tries to control and to keep in its proper place. Artificial stimulation of primitive trends obviously renders these more difficult to handle, and is certainly a contributing factor in minor forms of breakdown, anti-social acts, insanity and suicide. This is true also of the effect of constant scenes of violence and incredibly intense excitement repeatedly presented on films and television.

The widespread use of sedatives to relieve minor nerve strain, on the part of ordinary men and women, often obscures the results of such overstimulation, but adds another undesirable factor to the social picture. Some attempt at a more socially constructive use of these various media should therefore fall within the scope of preventive social hygiene.

It has also to be admitted that the medical profession, which as yet lacks adequate education in handling mental problems, tends too often to deal with patients suffering from mental distress only by means of physical drugs. Of these there are legion, and they have an undoubted place in the therapeutic field, somewhat as a life-saving apparatus can be used in emergency. But as with all things, while a moderate or temperate use of them is valuable, over-dosing or a too general application can produce conditions as regrettable as the disease itself.*

FURTHER FACTORS

In regard to human expectancy of life, medical knowledge and hygiene have decreased infant mortality to a remarkable extent, while longevity has increased at the other end of the normal span. Thus in many countries there is a large increase of population at the most vulnerable ages. Apart from any question of the over-crowding of the world by the increasing survival of many who would in other days have died, there is the question of the survival of the unfit, and an increase in diseases to be treated both in the young and in the old. Among children, the number of cripples and defectives in the community is growing, and there is also a greater preponderance of the diseases of old age—arteriosclerosis, degenerative diseases of the nervous system, cancer and so on. In other words, medical science keeps people alive, but it cannot always by any means keep them fit.

The picture may indeed appear discouraging, but needs to be faced so that both the medical professions and the public can be in a position to study the situation and assess its effect upon individual health. There is need, the writers strongly feel, for intelligent people to set themselves against artificialities at all levels and to make a stand—social as well as individual—for greater quiet in daily life; for natural and normally vital foodstuffs, grown in normally constituted soils; and for taking a consciously selective attitude towards activities which have now become automatic and indeed compulsive for a large proportion of mankind.

* See 'Tranquillising Drugs—A Critical Review', by James McC. Murdoch, M.R.C.P. (Edin.) in *The Pharmaceutical Journal*, April 20, 1957.

THE SOIL AND THE SEED

Account has so far been taken only of known and tangible factors in social medicine, but there are a number of others as to the cause of which medical science has no clue. Chief of these is the question of virus epidemics, since a relatively harmless virus can suddenly take on a lethal form for no apparent reason. Here, as with the larger bacteria, the tendency today is to consider the true cause of such infective diseases to reside less in the infective virus than in the conditions which favour its growth and virulence. In other words more importance is now ascribed to the 'soil' than to the 'seed'.

Sudden appearance of epidemic disease is considered by some eminent scientists, notably Mr J. E. R. McDonagh, F.R.C.S.,* to bear a relationship to cosmic rays, sun-spots and other sources of interstellar and interplanetary radiations. There is a considerable weight of scientific evidence to support this theory, and it can no longer be ignored or ridiculed.

THE DOCTOR-PATIENT RELATIONSHIP

The relationship between doctor and patient has had special characteristics since the very earliest times. The doctor of old was invariably a priest, and hence was looked upon as the channel between the aspect of deity said to be concerned with health and the petitioner asking to be healed. Even to-day something of that position still adheres to the physician or surgeon, even if he is an avowed materialist. He is felt to have more than normal knowledge; to be capable of taking charge of the sick and 'making them well'.

This is an important aspect of any healing work, and indeed in simple folk such faith plays a very great part in the doctor's capacity to 'do them good', for it enhances his ability to heal.

Apart from psychological projections from the patient, the doctor—because of his training and his wide acquaintance with disease conditions—brings into the situation significant factors

* See: 'The Nature of Disease Journal', Vol. II, page 149, Heinemann, London; 'The Universe in the Making', J. E. R. McDonagh, pages 21-23, Chaterson, London.   Also 'Presidential Address'. Royal Society of Medicine, Section on Comparative Medicine, 1954, by Sir Weldon Dalrymple-Champneys. Reported in *The Lancet*, October 30, 1954.

which contribute to the healing process. These are effective at least at the mental and psychological levels: if the doctor has also some realization of the spiritual aspects of his work, he can be the channel for vast healing influences. Such spiritual realization does not depend upon adherence to any cult or creed, but arises from or is associated with a quality of true human kindness, a sense of unity with one's fellow human beings and of dedication to their welfare. Such a quality of universality seems to open the way for a flow of healing power from the inner worlds, so that the very entrance of such a person into the room makes people 'feel better'.

Thus psychological conditioning in the patient, and certain factors in the physician which can only be called psychic or spiritual, combine to make the doctor-patient relationship both intricate and intimate. When these aspects of the relationship adjust themselves harmoniously in any given case, the doctor may be able to channel considerable healing power. This is undoubtedly one reason why the family doctor, whose function for a time tended to be overlooked or minimized, is now again recognized as having a significant place in personal and social medicine. He may not be intimately in touch with modern streamlined laboratory techniques, but he knows his people, and frequently understands them well, and so can often be more fundamentally successful in evoking creative readjustment than the highly technical specialist. Something 'sparks' between him and his patients, a new field of activity is created, and within that field subtle forces work that are powerful and real and directed towards fundamental healing. In the full doctor-patient relationship the whole nature of both is concerned, body, soul and spirit, and it is through a renewing sense of wholeness that true healing can best take place.*

The doctor has always to remember that there is often a *purposive* element in illness. Not infrequently an overstrained nervous system will develop a defensive disease for the sake of coping more effectively with its environment; or, in another type of person, as a means of avoiding the necessity for making any adaptation at all. While many practitioners are aware of this, there are also many others who miss the significance of a prolonged illness and lend themselves to a species of blackmail on the

* See 'Patients and Doctors', by Kenneth Walker, Chapter 8, Penguin Books Ltd.

part of the patient, who has chosen this method of securing his or her own way.

Present conditions in society and in the medical services have tended to loosen the sense of personal responsibility for health, as for so many other aspects of life. There is a current habit of saying 'I have caught' this or that disease, and to look only for sources of contagion. Yet it is quite clear that it is the patient himself who prepares the way for 'taking cold', etc., and that we do not fall ill unless we have provided a reason for it within ourselves.* The illness is in fact a projection of inner conflict or need at that time. Both doctor and patient will profit immensely by a recognition of this fact: our health is our own business and responsibility.†

The laws which govern health and the processes of healing are not so simple as some have imagined; they are admittedly not just those of the physical world nor concerned with physical treatment only. There can be and often are short-term physical healings of purely physical ailments, such as those caused by over-eating, acute fatigue, physical strain, sudden shock, etc. It is also true that crude animal health can co-exist with grave psychological disorders so long as the patient is unaware of the interior maladjustment and has no sense of conflict about it.

A block in the flow of vital forces may be caused by an external factor, as in a temporary tissue change such as a bruise; or by an internal factor, as in a psychological resistance of some sort. The physical block can easily be treated by ordinary physical methods, and failure to cure will occur only when the superficial condition is in some way linked to a deeper disorder. Palliative treatment, on the other hand, may give such relief that the interior disorder is influenced favourably, especially if the doctor-patient relationship is good, for then the psyche of the patient is eased by the attention bestowed. On the other hand, palliation may easily fail to be satisfactory if the deeper disorder is able to assert itself in spite of what is being done.

POSSIBILITIES AND LIMITATIONS

Certain very common conditions often militate against a satisfactory result. For example, there may be a lack of sympathetic

* See 'The Unknown Self', by Groddeck, C. W. Daniel & Co.
† See Appendix A, *Karma and Health*.

contact between doctor and patient, with the result that through distrust, dislike or confusion of mind the latter fails to benefit from the treatment prescribed. On the other hand the patient may withhold essential information, either through stupidity or some odd sense of cunning which seeks to test the doctor's insight or capacity to diagnose correctly. This leads to a confusion in the doctor-patient relationship which may prevent healing taking place.

In certain cases, the patient remains psychologically inaccessible, and the disease triumphs because he is unable to give the necessary co-operation. This may be due to a fundamental lack of appreciation on his part—or perhaps on the part of the doctor —that in effecting a cure *the ill person has as important a part to play as the doctor himself.* There are many people who expect a doctor to work a miracle without other help. There are others who have given up hope, and so never make any positive effort to recover; and yet others who, for deeply unconscious reasons, refuse entirely to get well because their illness serves some childish purpose such as keeping them in the limelight, calling forth sympathy, praise because of their courage, and so on. In all such cases the channel for spiritual healing is effectively blocked and little can be achieved.

Diagnosis, too, may at times, and for many reasons, be wholly mistaken. An osteopathic lesion for instance, may actually be the cause of acute headache, but, failing to recognize it, the doctor may prescribe aspirin instead of the needed manipulative treatment. So also, psychological disorders may remain undetected and the doctor continue treating symptoms when the basic trouble is the inability or unwillingness of the patient to make a real relationship with the world, or with that particular environment with which he is in contact.*

The same sort of errors may occur in treating psychological cases. An exponent of a special psychological method, such as scientology or dianetics, of which there are many to-day, may not realize the essentially hysterical character of the symptoms described by the patient, and so may apply his particular technique, such as it is, to a person on the verge of insanity, thereby tipping the patient over the border-line into a real psychosis.

From the point of view of that perennial philosophy from

* See Chapter V also.

which this study is approached, it may be presumed that all such incidents can be regarded as in some way working out the delicate balance of conditions in a patient's psychological field, leading him to just those contacts and the resulting treatments he may be said 'to deserve'. So also, when certain lessons have been learned that are related to the disease condition, a patient may be 'led'— or more accurately lead himself—to a doctor who is intuitive or sympathetic, or otherwise fitted to suggest or supply a really suitable cure for the given condition. It is a hard saying, but one with some depth of truth inherent in it, that there is often curative value in the persistent failure of external treatments.*

One must also accept the fact that deep-seated organic disease, involving tissue change, can rarely be entirely relieved. Changes in bodily tissues are subject to the effects of time, and if tissues have deteriorated beyond a certain point, the clock cannot be put back so that an old body becomes young, or a disorganized joint becomes smooth and effective again. In such cases, however, a true healing may arrest the deterioration, perhaps even bring decided improvement, and in any case will lead to the patient being inwardly serene in spite of his physical disabilities.

It has already been mentioned in this book that death itself may be regarded as a sign of a healing process having been accomplished; it should therefore not necessarily be looked upon as evidence of the failure of treatment. Of course, every member of the medical profession is bound by the Hippocratic oath to do all in his power to conserve the life as well as cure the illnesses of all patients who come to him, and failure to achieve this is regarded with regret. But for the embodied spirit the moment of death must in very many cases be one of release and satisfaction; while a long-continued fight against too heavy odds may often have taught the psyche much-needed and fundamental human lessons.†

Yet it remains true that sometimes a seemingly hopeless case makes a complete and miraculous recovery. The paradoxical thing is that in the rare instances when this occurs, it is often only after patient and doctor have given up hope. It seems as if the dropping of demand and expectancy, leading to an acceptance of things *as they are* and not as one would wish them to be, releases tension

---

* See Appendix A.

† See 'Some Unrecognized Factors in Medicine', Chapter II. Also 'Care of the Dying', by Ian Grant, M.B., *British Medical Journal*, December 28, 1957.

inside the patient, and even between the doctor and the patient. In this simpler situation, the healing forces have their chance to become effective.

In such cases, unexpected things can happen. Perhaps a new relationship comes into being between the patient and a new doctor, or the family pattern is changed by the death of some difficult member, or the return from abroad of a loved relative. Whatever the circumstances, the ultimate process will remain always that of a release of healing energy within the patient because the mind has ceased to bar its passage.

In short, in therapeutic work the relation between doctor and patient is of basic importance, and many failures are due to lack of understanding of this fact. But it should also be realized that the doctor himself may be only one factor in a larger pattern of relationships all of which affect the patient's attitude to life, and his willingness or otherwise to co-operate in healing himself.

*   *   *   *   *

Reviewing the medical outlook of to-day, one can say that while in some ways medical methods have made vast progress, in others they appear, from the spiritual viewpoint, to be regressive and moving away from deeper truth in favour of securing immediate results. But on the whole it would seem that medical thinking is tending towards a deeper and more integral view of sickness and of health, and nearer to the attitude which views the whole man, spiritual, psychic and physical, as the patient in need of help.

CHAPTER IV

OUTLINE OF HUMAN CONSTITUTION

> Humanistic culture is as important as natural scientific culture
> for the practice of medicine. As physicians we have to act upon
> men, and as man is body, mind, and spirit, we cannot limit
> ourselves to the study of the basic medical sciences ... we must
> take into consideration the human spirit, that mysterious power
> that makes us aware of our uniqueness, our liberty, our
> creativity, and directs us towards transcendent values.
>
> 'Lancet', September 21, 1957, *A. P. Cawadias*

IN the study of health and healing, the fundamental problem
is man, and his place in the scheme of things. It is therefore
impossible to understand the way in which psychic and spiritual
healing work, or fail to work, in different individuals and under
varying circumstances, without a fairly clear idea of the complicated nature of man. This subject will now be more fully considered.

According to the ancient teachings which form the background
of this book, man possesses a delicate and very complex organism
not only of his physical body, but even more so in the structure
and functioning of his interior consciousness. The interior consciousness is envisaged as having a mechanism for its expression at
its own level that is at least comparable with the physical organism,
although far more subtle and rapid in its changes of form. This
interior field of activity and the consciousness working through
it, is called the *psyche* in modern psychology, as it was by Plato
and St Paul. It covers the whole range of ordinary human thinking
and feeling, the individual psyche registering all the thoughts and
feelings that are experienced by any given personality. There is
also a highly sensitive connecting link between the psyche and the
physical body which has much to do with health and which will
be described later. Further, within and beyond the psyche lies a
still more interior centre of self-awareness and self-direction,
the possession of which distinguishes man from animals and
other non-human entities. It is human beings alone who are en-
dowed with this interior focus of will, and of spiritual perception.*

* Traditional descriptions of the constitution of man will be found in

In the traditional teachings, a human being is viewed primarily as this spiritual or transcendental entity. His roots lie deep in the Common Ground, in the one Life that is the source of all forms, as of all beings, and of all grades of consciousness. But the human being differs from other forms because he has a relatively permanent focus for his individual experiences. This is usually called the human spirit, or sometimes the spiritual Ego. It persists behind and through many incarnations upon earth, enjoying, rejecting, assimilating and growing through the experience gained in the restricted fields of personal life.*

Incarnation in a physical body necessitates for such a spiritual entity a somewhat complicated series of bridge mechanisms, or 'bodies', needed to bring the human spirit into effective and conscious touch with ponderous physical matter. The chief bridge between spirit and earth is that which we have called the psyche. It is the interior part of the psychosomatic, or body-mind organism that has been developed in the earlier kingdoms of nature, especially in the animal kingdom, for the later use and habitation of human Egos. This psychic and physical mechanism, when taken over by man, is naturally modified by its tenant, for during each human incarnation, each life in the physical world, it is his means of making contact with the psycho-physical field. Hence the psyche and the physical body of man, to-day, are characteristically human, expressing all that we now recognize as human characteristics. Yet because of its origin in the animal kingdom the psychosomatic organism is full of instinctual behaviour patterns—fear, self-preservation, sexual jealousy and the like—which are in essence sub-human.

'The Crest Jewel of Wisdom', by Sankaracharya, verses 89-109; and 'The Republic', by Plato, XIII and XXIV. 'Man, His Origins and Evolution', by N. Sri Ram, gives a modern presentation of the same material. Theosophical Publishing House, Adyar, Madras.

* There is a very ancient tradition that has been taught in most of the religions of the world, including early Gnostic Christianity, that the spirit of man gains in experience and wisdom by a series of human incarnations in the physical world until he has reached human perfection. Incarnation is then no longer necessary and further evolution takes place in the inner spiritual realms. This belief is assumed by the writers as being the most reasonable explanation of human existence.

See 'The Case for Reincarnation', by Leslie D. Weatherhead, D.D., Pebo, Speldhurst, Kent.

Direct psychic contacts and reactions, when these occur—as in dreams or in valid psychic experience—take place within the psyche and in relation to its own psychic field. This psychic field is objective, as real and factual at its own level as is the physical world, and having as wide a variation in vibratory rates. For modern research students, as for the ancient seers, the psychic field is beginning to be seen as a field of both personal and communal experience for all entities that think or feel, either consciously or in fixed patterns of behaviour, and this whole range of interior experience, subtle and evanescent as it is, is now recognized as subject to laws which can be ascertained. The field is normally composed of the vibratory rates of thought and feeling, though other forces play through it from time to time. It consists, as noted above, of the intermediate range of reactivity that lies between the spiritual world and the phenomena known to physical science.

Thus the psychological element in each human being, his psyche, has a dual function. It is for the spiritual man the direct intermediary between his spiritual consciousness and the psychic field of which it is a part; and it also acts as a bridge for the play of the spiritual consciousness through to dense physical experience.

The effect of thought and feeling upon physical health and behaviour is nowadays freely admitted. Physical well-being, manners and habitual behaviour, all continually reflect the impress of unseen determinants. Interior patternings such as those of anxiety or fear, are unconsciously—but very faithfully—carried down to the physical organism from the psychological level. Habitual thought and feeling patterns exist at the interior level, acting automatically there, just as the organs of digestion act automatically within the physical frame. Being so much below, or within, the normal level of awareness, and yet in the direct·line of the flow of life from within outwards, it is easy to see how, entirely without our knowing it, interior states of mind and feeling can stimulate, depress, or even disorganize, automatic functions of the body such as breathing, digestion, or glandular secretions.

Always behind both body and psyche lies the still semi-conscious life of the spiritual man, later to become more fully conscious and to take charge of the whole range of human experience. But for most people the life of the spirit is known only in occasional flashes, often under pressure of circumstances as in an emergency, or when the attention has been trained to evoke it by some form of self-directed discipline.

Let us before going further review this picture of man.

To awaken the powers of the latent spiritual consciousness, it is necessary that this consciousness be brought into contact with the impacts of dense physical nature. Hence the human spirit is provided with vestures* within each of the main fields that are now recognized as the background of human existence.

These fields are here given as three: (a) the home of the creative spirit, which responds to impulses of abstract ideation, of compassion and unity, and of pure will; (b) the psychic or soul world which has been explored by modern psychologists, and from earliest times by those seeking spiritual experience; and (c) the physical world, in all its variations.

To the student of the perennial philosophy none of these fields is simple, either in structure or in the forces that act through it. Over and above their human inhabitants, each has elements that tend to stimulate life and to build forms, and each has non-human denizens as varied as those we recognize in the physical world.

Further, the ancient teachings include an aspect of the physical body that is not as yet fully recognized in the West, although it is beginning to be suspected that it must exist. Eastern physiologists and yogis concern themselves very much with a force known as *prana*, or vital energy. At the physical level it may be recognized as vitality, or physical vital energy, permeating every cell and every tissue. Although closely allied to nervous energy, it is nevertheless distinct. There are in fact many varieties of prana, or vitality, each with its peculiar characteristics, but a full study of these is outside the purpose of this book.† This power is not electrical in nature, although it has much in common with electricity. Its quality is more like that of the strong magnetic field associated with electrical phenomena, and it is only fair to say that its reactions being so involved with the actual electrical charges in the body, it is a most difficult problem to disentangle the two forces and to see each independently. Yet the recognition

---

* 'God made coats of skins and clothed them', Genesis III, 21.

† It has been known as orgone, odic fluid, Mesmeric fluid, etc. See 'Letters on Od and Magnetism', Reichenbach. Hutchinson & Co.

of this life force (prana) as a specific phenomenon in nature, would do much to help solve problems that continue to puzzle the biologist, who is naturally confused by the close interaction of vital and electrical energies in the same field.*

Taken as a whole, this energizing life-force—before its differentiation and specialization for use in the bodies of man— is solar in origin. It is the basic principle underlying life processes throughout the whole of the organic structure of nature.

In the human kingdom each individual appropriates and modifies solar prana and passes it on in a specialized form to his appropriate 'body' at each level of awareness. Thus each 'body'— spiritual, psychic and physical—is 'fed' at its own level. If there is a free interaction between consciousness and its environment, then the power of the subtler nature in man is such that this interior life-force can, and often does, sustain the physical body when its physical energy would normally be totally exhausted.

The nature and functions of the vital forces in man have been discussed at some length in previous publications.† Here only a bare outline of man's vital organism can be given. The most important fact is that the two-way flow of vital energy constitutes a subtle bridge by which conditions in the psyche contact and affect the functions and behaviour of the dense physical frame. The pranic flow partakes of the nature both of the denser levels of the psychic world and of the finer constituents of the physical world, and so enables the two to interact intimately. It responds readily to thought and to feeling, and yet it can act as matrix for changes in dense physical cell life. It is indeed the missing link in the current problem of psycho-somatic reactions.

In addition, a somewhat dense vital energy‡ appears to be anchored to the cells of every tissue, and tends to reflect the state of the physical tissues with which it is associated, registering fatigue, congestion, wounds, etc., as well as good health. The finer, free-flowing stream of vitality is continually passing through the whole of the body, and the static and free moving types interplay with each other.

A point of great interest for us in this particular study is that

---

* See 'Fields of Force', Duncan. Theosophical Publishing House, London.

† See 'Some Unrecognized Factors in Medicine', Chapter III, under 'The Etheric Body; and 'Man Incarnate', by P. D. and L. J. Bendit, M.D. Theosophical Publishing House, London.

‡ Usually called dense etheric matter in modern occult text books.

the circulation of the subtler prana is heavily conditioned by the habitual attitude of the psyche. Static vitality is more influenced by food, correct metabolism, exercise, fatigue, and other physical influences ordinarily associated with physiological health. But the flow of the subtler prana is from within outwards, and is immediately influenced by thought and feeling.

The static vitality in any living form, plus its free flowing prana, are currently called its etheric or vital body. And it is the etheric body as a whole that forms the bridge mechanism for the transmission of suggestion, conscious or unconscious, since it responds directly and automatically to any change in psychological attitude. Thus both tradition and repeated re-observation provide a rationale of psychological healing, because such healing, in releasing fixations, tensions, etc., thereby frees the flow of interior, revitalizing forces.

The present physical form of man is the result of vast and lengthy evolutionary experiment. Owing to the development of the sensitive structures such as the brain and nervous systems, the human body can be trained to express something of the creative life of a self-aware spiritual entity. Scientists now state that the human race is the only species that can be said still to be evolving*
—that is, developing new capacities. The ancient teachings would claim that this is because man is still on the whole very imperfect. He is expressing his psyche—a very considerable range of thought and feeling—but his finer spiritual self is still almost completely hidden for the major part of his life. Potentially man is a fully self-aware entity, but he has taken over his form from the kingdom below him, and is still conditioned by its automatic behaviour. He shares the field of thought and feeling, as he shares the physical world, with other sentient creatures, although the latter will always move through these fields rather automatically, urged by innate instinctual patterns and group automatisms. Man alone of all the denizens of these worlds, seen and unseen, is capable of becoming fully aware of them all and of himself in relation to them.

The psyche of a human being of our western racial type, as we have said, is a compound of accumulated reactions from the animal past and the emerging creative consciousness. Most of

* See 'Evolution in Action', Julian Huxley. Chatto & Windus, London, 1953, pp. 130-2.

man's life works on patterns that are firmly established, many of them acting automatically below the surface of conscious thought. Yet the individual psyche, that subtle, personal 'field' of combined thought and emotion, is held together by the continuity of its attachment to the spirit of the man, and is the personal link between that spirit and its physical form, for the duration of each physical incarnation. Even after the death of the physical body the psyche persists, for a time which varies according to type and development, and then gradually its experiences are absorbed or 'digested' by the individual consciousness, its spiritual Root.

THREE-FOLD ACTIVITY OF PSYCHE

In an ordinary human being the psyche or soul has in itself a three-fold activity, determined by the various qualities and combinations of the material of which it is composed, and the uses to which it is put.

Virtually all normal people have the possibility of a conscious, even if limited, contact with the eternal spirit which is their inmost centre and essence. The contact may be dim, confused, uncertain, but it exists. This is the upper range of the psyche's reactivity, the field of unselfish emotion and impersonal thought, and it can be reinforced and strengthened, or starved and impoverished. It is the field of all true creative thought and feeling, and a spear-point of growth towards spiritual awareness.

The average human being has also a well-developed middle field of feeling-thought experience, usually with the two elements inextricably interwoven and very largely unconscious, although they operate with strength and fixity in determining the behaviour of the person. Here lie the complicated thought-feeling mechanisms of personal relationships, social and personal aspirations, fears, desires—indeed all the 'habit-formations' of the psychologist.*. When latent, the patterns shrink to tiny nuclei, but at a touch of some outer or interior stimulus they rush into activity again. This is the typical 'soul' of man, a half-way house between spirit and body, heavily leaning upon the physical world, because that supplies a perennial stimulus to mind and to emotion. Only by the deliberate reversal of attention and some training can man

* See 'Some Unrecognized Factors in Medicine', 2nd Edition, pp. 55-69. Also 'Matter, Mind and Man', by E. W. Sinnott. Harper.

find stimuli of equal power at the level of the eternal spirit. So, for most people, the physical world is 'real' and the within is vague, illusory, almost unknown.

The densest level of the psyche is that which is most closely connected with the physical world. Here sensory reports and commands from the inner man flow back and forth, through a two-way traffic system of vital energies. This latter follows with great accuracy the actual nerve structures of the dense physical nervous system and the brain. The lines of communication have their co-ordinating centre in the pituitary area (hypothalamus) of the brain, so far as the body is concerned, but conscious co-ordination is directed from the subtler areas of the psyche rather than by the brain itself.*

Behind the complicated mechanisms of the body, and behind the threefold levels of the psyche itself, it is the spirit in man, and the spirit alone, that 'knows'. That is, it is the spiritual man alone who can record any new experience, take any original action, or think any original thought. The psyche is almost entirely automatic, governed by habit and unconscious motivations, repeating reactions in well-worn grooves, until challenged by the Spirit.

This fact is of very deep importance in all healing, because patients are inclined to think that anything 'new', any fresh impulse towards health or change, must come from outside themselves. The contrary is equally, if not more true, especially for those with a highly sensitized nature. A fresh point of view presented by a friend or a practitioner may apparently change the behaviour of the patient, bringing hope or relief from anxiety. But—as all practitioners know only too well—nothing one can say or do can touch a psyche that is in complete retreat, one that is, as it is termed, 'inaccessible'. The patient hears, but remains darkened, because the spirit within is shut behind some locked door of retreat, resistance, or despair, and seems unable to break through to clearer vision, or respond to outer stimulus. If such a spirit can be aroused or contacted, through mental or spiritual healing, through shock, or by prayer and deep spiritual identification on the part of the healer, then and then only will the patient's

* See 'Study in Consciousness', by A. Besant, Chapter IX; and 'Cerebral Cortex and the Mind of Man', Wilder Penfold in 'The Physical Basis of Mind'. Blackwell.

mind apply itself to the 'new' idea, and make a fresh, constructive approach.

It is therefore always the life of the spirit that heals, and that *can* heal, if it can be released. Apart from the care of the physical body, with suitable remedies, rest, etc., to assist its recovery as a physical entity, the problem of the healer is almost always one of the adjustment and release of tension at the mental-emotional level.

This is of course expecially true in a long-continued illness where a habit formation has been strongly developed in the psyche, and it is also profoundly true in mental disease.

Even a momentary sense of wholeness at the psychological level can be restorative—sometimes surprisingly so. The condition known spiritually as a 'state of grace' may be envisaged as a temporary obliteration of the distortions of the psyche, so that spiritual life-force flows unimpeded from within outwards. If the distortions are not actually obliterated, or pushed aside, there may be a temporary synchronicity, an alignment of consciousness into something like harmony between the different levels, and—while that lasts—at least a temporary miracle of cure could take place. Whether the original condition of disease is permanently cured; or returns, slowly reasserting itself; or reappears immediately the excitement of the moment is over, will depend in part on the degree to which the disease has affected the physical tissues, but chiefly upon the patient and his capacity to make use of his healing experience.

The purpose of healing practices is usually merely the restoration of normal reactions in the physical body, but the above outline will show how much is actually involved in securing such a result. It also shows the necessity to approach the subject of healing, as well as the practice of medicine, with an understanding of man's psyche and of his spiritual nature as the foundation upon which all true cures are in fact established.

CHAPTER V

THE PSYCHOLOGICAL APPROACH
TO HEALING

A man's body and his mind, with the utmost reverence to both
I speak it, are exactly like a jerkin and a jerkin's lining: rumple
the one, you rumple the other.
'Life and Opinions of Tristram Shandy', *Sterne*

The mind is its own place, and in itself
Can make a Heav'n of Hell, a Hell of Heav'n.
'Paradise Lost', *Milton*

MODERN PSYCHOSOMATIC MEDICINE

FROM the point of view of this study, all chronic systemic diseases are psychosomatic. This is to say that the cause of disharmony in the body is an *interior* disharmony, registering as physical disease, or ill-health; the psychic and somatic elements thus appearing as two sides of a single entity.* With increasing frequency, medical circles are recognizing that physical disorders which resist attempts at treatment may often have their origin in the psyche, and are not accessible to physical treatment alone. The association of peptic ulcers with sudden mental shock, or prolonged anxiety, is well established, while many cases of chronic colitis are known to have a psychological origin. Similarly, severe malfunctions of the heart, chronic skin diseases, and general muscular weakness are often traced to emotional conflict, and can only be cured by resolving the latter.

The situation, in all such cases, is that the disease acts as a safety valve for some otherwise unbearable tension at the thought-feeling level. The symptoms produced are then termed conversion symptoms, for the disease takes the place of the problem and causes less distress to the patient than would be the case if the inner difficulty were faced or acknowledged. Such difficulty may lie within the patient, as when a personal characteristic is repugnant to him; or it may lie outside in his environment, for example when work or companions are deeply uncongenial.

* See 'Some Unrecognised Factors in Medicine', Chapter IV.

These situations are not uncommon, and when a patient becomes ill rather than face a difficulty, it is only a special example of the general principle that all disease is purposive. Such a disease is merely a crude, instinctual way of drawing attention to, or turning attention away from, situations, conditions, and relationships, with which the patient feels unable to cope. His incapacity may be due to his ignorance of some fundamental law, or to inability to use resources that lie at his command. It is as unintelligent as trying to hide by shutting one's eyes when pursued— but the fact remains that such disease is often an effective way of relieving the patient from the necessity of facing, or dealing with, unpleasant situations.*

The symptoms developed will naturally vary with the psychological type and the stage of development of the individual, as well as with the condition of his physical body and its flow of vital energy. Here such factors as debility, sunlight, sleep, exercise, and vitamins, play their recognized parts, and hence *at times* purely physical treatment—such as change of diet, a course of medicine, physiotherapy, or an osteopathic adjustment—will relieve the physical symptoms of psychosomatic disease. As examples one may cite allergies manifesting as skin trouble, asthma, or migraine, which often yield to drug treatment, avoidance of specified foods, or suitable spinal adjustment. More often they require treatment from a psychotherapist, who is usually to be found on the staff of the larger hospitals, and who will seek the interior cause of evident nervous tension. In favourable cases a cure may be established after only a single consultation, though in most cases the deeply seated nature of the disturbance will need a number of interviews.

Sometimes a more subtle situation arises, when skin troubles or digestive disturbances in small children are found to be due to anxieties in their parents. Psychological tensions are often picked up unconsciously by the children, even though care may have been taken to hide such worries from them. Racial and industrial tensions also can produce maladjustments that register in certain diseases, or tendencies to disease. So the list of illnesses recognized as psychosomatic grows larger from year to year.

* See 'The Unknown Self', by Groddeck. C. W. Daniel and Co.

ANALYTICAL TECHNIQUES

Psycho-analysis and its later derivatives represent one of the great modern advances in the study of mental disease, because they have restored to the field of serious study material which had for a time been ignored as being irrelevant and of no value. The analytical techniques have now shown that irrational processes, such as dreams, slips of the pen and tongue, and unconscious actions, reveal conditions existing below the surface of the mind which fit into an organized and purposeful, even if unconscious, system of thought and feeling. Such patterns belong to a mind ill at ease and in conflict with itself which, by means of overt symptoms, attempts both to restore a balance and to draw the attention of the conscious individual to the existence of the hidden conflict.

The symptoms may remain purely mental and emotional, in which case the illness is called neurosis; or they may reflect into the physical organism and produce one of the ever-growing group of illnesses termed psychosomatic.

Moreover, the psychoanalytic movement has opened our eyes to the way the more serious forms of mental disease—i.e. insanity or psychosis—arise from milder disorders, and occur when the higher aspects of consciousness increasingly lose control over the personality. We now also know that if therapeutic measures can be applied in the early stages of mental conflict, the tensions may be resolved and true health restored.

The general principle underlying all analytical techniques is that of bringing matters which are hidden or ignored into the field of consciousness, and thus making the patient aware of the nature of his symptoms and of their relationship with underlying conflicts due to fear, guilt, frustration, ambition and the like. It is obvious that to do this with any degree of success there must be willingness on the part of the patient (a) to face the less pleasant and more shadowy aspects of himself, and (b) to co-operate with, and in some measure to trust, the therapist with whom he has agreed to work.

The first requirement is necessary because—consciously or unconsciously—one is always anxious to think of oneself in a good light, and to conceal from oneself and from others the pettiness, and what one considers to be the 'ugliness' or the 'impurity' in one's own character. Thus one's 'shadow', as Jung calls it, is kept out of sight, hidden even from oneself. It is interesting that the Roman Church, with its emphasis on confession, shows a realization of the need to face this hidden or darker self.

Co-operation with the therapist is essential because, as we have said, the actual healing process can only take place in a common psychic field. Where this exists there is said to be a good rapport between the patient and the therapist.*

At the present time there are many schools, each using its own characteristic technique, and each having a different view of the symptoms revealed. We are concerned here only with general principles, so will divide these schools roughly into two groups: (1) those that look backward into the history of the individual for the cause of his troubles; and (2) those that look forward and think in teleological terms. There is an intermediate group, which concerns itself with immediate problems—such, for example, as may arise out of a broken marriage—but this, while it often deals effectively with relatively superficial and immediate matters, does not aim at profound readjustments or at character re-education.

The first group works on reductive lines. It looks into the past, exploring the patient's childhood and seeking the cause of his disturbance in terms of repression. Its practitioners deal with the primitive, instinctual nature of man and child, and with the divisions and conflicts that arise within that nature, as well as between the rational individual and his instincts. They are frequently successful in relieving symptoms, but offer no direct assistance in positive character development. It is true that the individual who has been thus analysed often alters his behaviour, but this is due more to the release of pressure and anxiety than to anything learned about conscious integration. There is indeed a natural urge in every human being to move forward toward spiritual fulfilment, which may be released during this form of analysis. But it can likewise happen—and indeed has happened—that what is set free under reductive analysis is destructive and disruptive, so that from the social point of view the last state of the patient is worse than the first.

It is not always realized that people of considerable spiritual stature may still have patches of unassimilated past experience

---

* The projection by the patient of an habitual or unfulfilled emotional relationship into this field, so that the analyst is felt to be a father or a mother, etc., is usually called the transference, *vide infra*.

within their natures which may be dark and ugly. If these are released and brought to the surface of the conscious mind through deep analysis, some positive technique of assimilation, control or transformation should be communicated at the same time, so that the patient may deal with the material constructively, rather than fall under its domination. A conscious contact with some higher octave of his being is necessary in order to effect such a transformation, and such spiritual contact can only be evoked by each individual from within himself. An analyst who is in touch with his own spiritual nature—to whatever school he belongs—can be an effective agent in arousing in his patient an awareness of latent self-directive power. On the other hand, one who lacks such interior experience may release forces in a patient over which neither he nor his patient appear to have any control.

The second group of therapists, like the first, is concerned with the primitive and instinctual nature of the patient, but sees this as a fount of energy which, from the human point of view, needs not only to be set free from its old automatisms but to be harnessed creatively to human and spiritual ends. Hence, to this school, the process of analysis is incomplete unless the patient is not merely relieved of his symptoms, but is at the same time taught to find his way towards a realization of his true nature, and hence towards an integration of his personality. The weakness of the practitioners of this group—of which Jung's school of analytical psychology is the most notable example—is that its exponents may be so much concerned with the spiritual and the teleological aspects of the patient's problem, that they fail to deal effectively with his primitive and instinctual nature. It has been said of them that although under their treatment the patient may develop a new philosophy of life, the original symptoms frequently remain untouched.

While certain schools minimize the importance of the influence which the analyst exerts over the mind of his patient, others recognize frankly that the analyst-patient relationship is the operative factor in this form of treatment. Even the analyst of the old school, sitting behind a screen in darkness, actually impresses the mind of his patient with his own mental patterns. From the point of view of those making this study, it is the fact of the existence of the common mental field, built up between therapist and patient, that explains why practitioners of so many schools do apparently cure patients suffering from similar difficulties, although each group would describe the mental mechanism by which the cure had been produced in utterly different, indeed often incompatible, terms.

The success of the intermediate group, which concerns itself chiefly with symptom-analysis, is probably due to the result of a harmonious fusion of the patient's mind with that of the analyst. This results in a release of tension, and a loss of the sense of guilt or of anxiety in some form, whether the psychological interpretation given to the patient is or is not wholly sound. It is not, however, just the soothing syrup of a good relationship that brings about a lasting cure, but some element of enlightenment, or truthfulness, that illumines the patient's mind and enables him to make a successful conscious readjustment.

It is clear that while an analyst cannot 'carry' a patient further than he has gone himself, a patient may sometimes be able to use the analyst-patient relationship as a stepping stone to a perception of reality beyond that which the analyst himself possesses. In such cases the practitioner acts as a catalyst—producing results by his presence, and by such knowledge as he is able to exhibit.

Like every real healer, a good analyst has that quality for which Jung uses the word *mana*; the Hindu would call it *shakti*. The word implies a contact with an interior centre of life which is not only a source of power but also a centre of stability, an interior point of reference. Patients may be either attracted or repelled by the sense of 'power' that emanates from a good analyst, and this reaction needs to be carefully distinguished from other intimate elements in the patient-analyst relationship. A patient may be favourably predisposed to a certain analyst solely because of the latter's attractive personality, or a superficial likeness to someone else. The opposite is also true. Repulsion may be due to actual incompatibility of temperament, or on the other hand to the challenge to old habits of thought and feeling represented by the therapist.

In a sense it is true that the practitioner's private life has nothing to do with the patient, or with the therapeutic relationship. Nevertheless, since that life is part of the whole personality of the therapist, he cannot leave it outside his consulting room. So a fastidious patient may quite genuinely be repelled by a practitioner whose private life is coarse and sensual, even though the latter may be highly skilled and ethical in his professional work.

A clarification of the intimate factors so far discussed, in regard to the patient-analyst relationship, will do much to promote a successful outcome of any treatment, the practitioner being then used consciously as catalyst, not necessarily accepted as confessor or spiritual guide.

Valuable—and indeed in many cases, indispensable—as an analyst may be, the key to all psychological and psychosomatic therapy lies, as we have so often said, within the patient himself. In one sense the therapeutic factor is remote and unconscious, lying in the little used spiritual centre of the individual. But from another point of view, successful and radical psychotherapy depends upon the fact of bringing an automatic and unconscious process of thought or feeling into the clear light of conscious judgment, because this submits it directly to a transformatory process.

It follows from this that, despite the value of an external therapist and of the rapport between him and the patient, true psychotherapy can, and frequently does, occur in an individual working within and by himself. The cure then takes place as a sequel to a moment of insight, of clear perception, when the person suddenly sees himself as reacting automatically and needlessly to some particular situation. Such a realization of his own compulsive behaviour puts him in a position to choose whether in future he will go on behaving in that way. Obviously if the reaction is painful or shameful, he will be ready enough to give it up if he can. But it sometimes happens that the symptom is in some way useful, or gives the patient a sense of importance, so that a weak character may cling to it, even while partially realizing that he is himself creating it to his own detriment.

In all psychological work it is now well known that recovery from deep-seated or long established neurotic conditions takes time. Miracles do sometimes happen: sudden release from compulsive behaviour does occur, but needs close watching, lest deeper layers of the disorder not yet touched reassert themselves.

The levels at which integration takes place vary, and may affect the whole psyche in one sequence or another. Emotional release, deliberate or accidental, can lead to a change of ideas; a rational perception of the possibility of a new outlook, of a wider view upon life, can react into emotional readjustment; and at the deeper layers of awareness, a sudden or slowly emerging contact with spiritual reality can release a sense of power, or freedom from guilt, or an outburst of forgiveness of injury, which profoundly influences both habits and character. Religious conversions, when genuine, are of this nature.

For sound readjustment to take place all that is needed is an experience of integration *within one's own field of consciousness*. Circumstances may not alter, the situation may be as difficult as it was before, but if the patient has found a new orientation to his own inner nature, the symptoms that constitute his illness need no longer persist. Little by little, layer by layer, he will find new freedom within himself. If this works out into a change in his environment, well and good, but he need no longer be ill or unhappy.

Other less fortunate people—possibly less adventurous natures —cannot or will not reach out of their own volition into new fields of experience, either outer or inner. For them the conscious naming of their trouble is not enough, and for these some form of active therapy is often found to be useful. Even a somewhat compulsive or enforced occupation can serve this purpose—some routine that necessitates the formation of fresh associations, such as a change of occupation, or the regular exercise of the mind in study. Such forms of active therapy are not advised as often as one might expect, possibly because it is generally thought that *conscious* readjustment is the only means of cure.

Yet the gradual building up of the power of self-direction through learning a new technique of some sort, however simple, has profound therapeutic value, which does not seem to be fully appreciated at present. Reorientation is supposed to arrive, from within, as a result of bringing hidden patterns of thought and feeling to the surface of consciousness. In some instances it does so arrive—but in others it does not. In the latter case, some form of *directed* activity, even if compulsorily performed, may help to break up established automatic behaviour, and bring about a new orientation.

From the point of view here presented, one of the most important things that can happen in psychological treatment is the discovery of volition, of the power of the inner man to take charge, and to choose deliberately to think and act in ways that are more constructive than the old behaviour patterns. If the knowledge comes of itself, through insight, well and good; and if not, it can at times be induced by the practice of one or other type of active therapy, or of some form of religious discipline, used with aspiration and intelligent understanding of its purpose.

The whole subject of integration very easily runs over into the religious field, for there are various levels at which the integrative process works. Recovery from distressing symptoms may be due to a changed mental attitude, or to the discarding or outgrowing of an emotional need. Each of these would bring a slight integration of personality, with greater freedom or greater control of thought or feeling. But there is also a progressive experience, arriving as the result of a successful analysis, which may go on for years, as insight increases and is applied to deeper levels of the psyche. Sooner or later this experience of progressive integration merges into some form of religious or philosophic enlightenment. As progressive enlightenment takes place, the inner life is more and more vividly realized, and the laws of the spiritual life, individual and social, may be increasingly understood.

HYPNOSIS AND SUGGESTION

Hypnosis and suggestion are two forms of therapy usually linked together and, indeed, there is no hard and fast line between them. While it is at least theoretically possible for a person to be hypnotised against his will, in practice this is rarely the case. It has in fact been denied that hypnosis can take place without the consent of the subject, though it is true that such consent may be indirect or tacit.

From the psychic viewpoint it appears that suggestion depends on the passage of ideas from mind to mind, and then from the mind of the recipient into his physical vital field. Hypnosis, on the other hand, involves a direct assault upon the patient's vital field, and hence does not depend primarily on any mental interchange, or suggestion, although this also is usually present.

This distinction may seem arbitrary, but if we realize that the hypnotist always induces 'sleep' or 'trance' by the use of physical methods, the matter becomes clearer. These physical methods range from using only a particular tone of voice, cajoling or imperative, to a general attack on the physical organism by means of fatigue, starvation, threats, torture, etc., such as is too often used by the authorities in autocratic countries. Most often, in medicine, the voice and some simple objects like a bright light, or a metronome, or 'passes' with the hand, are used to put the patient under the over-riding influence of the operator.

When suggestion is successful there is a willing acceptance of certain ideas put forward by the practitioner: in hypnosis there is an imposition of the practitioner's idea on the passive mind of the patient. This, however, is usually done subsequent to a more or less prolonged use of suggestion, and it is because of this blending that no clear clinical distinction between the two is to be found in most books on the subject. Yet there *is* such a distinction when the processes are considered from the viewpoint of this book.

Suggestion actually is a factor which is potent in everyday life. Willy-nilly, if we hear a thing said often enough, it produces an influence on our minds. This may be positive or negative, so that the advertisement which reiterates that 'X is good for you' may induce a person to think that he must buy and use X; or, if the reader has strong views as to the harmfulness of certain things, it may rouse a contrary feeling, a resistance to considering whatever good points X may really have. In either case, suggestion is at work: the mind of the advertiser is affecting that of the reader or listener. A link has been made between mind and mind, and over it certain notions are carried, leading to acceptance or rejection.

It is not always realized, however, that there is much truth in the fact that the bottle of medicine, however effective it may be in itself because of its contents, really bears out in some measure the view that 'It may be coloured water, but it works just the same'. Some at least of the efficacy of the medicine depends upon its suggestive element—a fact once pointed out by Sir Walter Langdon-Brown in a discussion on fashions in prescribing. He emphasized the fact that when a doctor believes in, or is interested in, the remedy he prescribes, the results are better than when he is doubtful or indifferent. The effect, moreover, is enhanced by the fact that a patient coming to a doctor is usually already in a state of mind to listen to what he is told and to accept the doctor's views. If he is not, he would do better to go elsewhere and find another physician in whom he believes.

This gives the key to the whole process of suggestion used as a therapeutic measure. For it depends on establishing a rapport between physician and patient at the mental level. All that has been said in the previous section about the patient-analyst relationship is important in this connection also. The doctor uses such rapport to put certain ideas into the patient's mind with the purpose of helping him towards a restoration of health, mental or physical.

For treatment to be successful the prime need is the willingness of the patient to receive these ideas. Such willingness need not be either direct or conscious. Equally, the refusal to accept may lie below the conscious level, or behind apparent agreement on the part of the patient—yet failure will ensue.

Assuming, however, that the patient is truly willing, the effect of the suggestion is to change the thought and feeling currents in his mind, and this in turn releases tensions in the vital field, or restores to it a tone which it has lost. Where physical disease is concerned, this restoration of tone may influence the actual tissues concerned and bring them back to a healthy state. Moreover, if the suggestion goes deep enough gradually to re-educate the patient, so that he begins to feel and think differently about life, he may come into touch with new energies of a spiritual order within himself, which will thereafter enable him to maintain a better standard of health than before, and even to cure himself should he later become ill. The process has then passed far beyond the level of suggestion and become something quite different, being now a form of spiritual auto-therapy.

Thus suggestion can be highly effective. Its exact form is not always the same. Sometimes the quiet reassurance resulting from the feeling that something is being done to help, may be enough to set a frightened patient on the way to health. At other times suggestive help may have to be much more specific, and directed towards teaching the patient to think, feel or act differently towards a particular symptom, while the doctor stands by him until the new habit is firmly established.

There are, however, certain criteria in the use of suggestion, apart from the willingness or unwillingness of the patient to accept what he is told. One of these is truth: there must be a realistic approach to the problem presented by the disease. It is no use telling a sick person that he is getting better unless he is, or that he has no illness when he is suffering—even if the suffering be only at the mental level. Lack of truth and realism frustrate the deepest forms of therapy. Something in the patient will reject the suggestions made; and even if results are achieved, these will probably be neither deep nor permanent.

On the other hand, positive, dynamic suggestion may help

even serious disease—provided the therapist believes what he says. Thus, to say, 'Yes, you are ill, but you can get better' is an attitude which can do no harm and may do much good. On the contrary, to say 'You are not really ill' may lead, if accepted with one part of the patient's mind, to suppression and deletion of the symptoms of disease, the root remaining as before, so that his last state is worse than the first.

Hypnosis is a method of therapy which is not to be commended. It involves the imposition of the will of one personality on another, with the result that the subject's hold on himself, and particularly on his vital etheric field, is weakened. Dissociation may be produced, so that although pains and fears vanish from sight, the cause of them is not removed. Thus, even when teeth are extracted under hypnosis, or a mother bears a child without conscious discomfort, the nervous system may retain the effect of shock in a manner it does not when proper anaesthesia has been used.

In the psychiatric field, too, the results of hypnosis are not good except under one condition, as pointed out years ago by Dr William Brown; that is, where the patient with amnesia is helped, under hypnosis, to remember the 'lost' memories. A wise use of hypnosis can lead such a patient to become better integrated and more difficult to hypnotize as time goes on: precisely the opposite of what happens when hypnosis is used for other purposes, serious or frivolous.

Loss of self-directive power by a hypnotized subject is due to the fact that when one person hypnotizes another, something of the operator's own etheric material is projected into the etheric field of the subject. The operator's vital energies displace those of the subject, and hence may bring about disorganization of the vital forces and a weakening of the subject's control over himself.

Moreover, despite the strong suggestion which reputable hypnotists put to the patient, that the latter will be independent of them at the end of the course of treatment, the integrity of the vital field is not always fully restored, and the breach may not be healed for some time afterwards. In other words, the patient may give the appearance of integrity, but has not really recovered it.

It is evident that if a doctor—or other person—wishes to hypnotise a subject, the process will be very much facilitated by the establishment of close personal rapport in the first instance.

Following this, a gradual increase of confidence is established between the two, the suggestion becomes stronger, and the patient increasingly willing to fall in with what the doctor indicates. And if it be suggested that he fall asleep, he is prepared to do so. If, then, some physical impact is made, such as a word of command, or if the eyes are strained by focussing them on a light, the already receptive etheric field of the patient is open to the influence of the hypnotist *at that level*, as well as at the mental level where the relationship has already been made and developed.

In short, hypnotism is a form of therapy which, seen from the psychic standpoint, is undesirable. If a gap in consciousness has to be filled in, it is probably much safer in extreme cases to do this by the use of impersonal drugs and 'narco-analysis',* as this makes the personal mingling of fields unnecessary, and the breach in the psychic field of the subject is more easily healed.

Autosuggestion. There is a third form of mental suggestive treatment known as autosuggestion. Many contend that this is merely an extension of the hetero-suggestive process. When one reads in a book or learns from another how to give oneself help by constructive thinking, the process has actually been initiated from the outside, and all the patient does is to carry on this process, started by another, with variations according to his temperament. For example, one can say to oneself, 'This is a dark hall but I am not frightened of dark halls any more, because I know the cause of the fear in my childhood and it no longer affects me as it used to do'. That is a mental suggestion, an idea 'learned' from another, and may have more or less effect according to the circumstances of the learning. It can well be a purely mental or verbal statement and will then prove fundamentally ineffective. Such verbal repetition of phrases which state that circumstances are as you wish them to be, is a popular notion of auto-suggestion. It has genuine dangers, such as superficiality, insincerity, self-delusion, and the like.

There is another form of autosuggestion, better called auto-therapy, which is radically different from any such exercise. The

---

* *Narco-analysis* is analysis when the patient is under the influence of a mild narcotic which temporarily inhibits the action of the higher centres of consciousness. The patient becomes only partially conscious, but is able to answer questions with less reticence and resistance than usual. In this way the root of a problem can sometimes be uncovered more easily than when the patient is fully conscious.

technique induces the person who uses it to reach back, deep within himself, and there make contact with his own centre of interior experience, and thus with the renewing power of the one Life, the Common Ground. From such a contact both a sense of release and a realization of interior healing power can flow out to mind, feelings and body. While the technique of such an experience can be taught, its practice is experimental, and not everyone can use it. It is an individual matter, and its final effect has little to do with anyone save the person using the exercise.

The practice begins with deep conscious relaxation, not to induce a self-hypnotic state, but to ease nerve tensions. It is undertaken with full conscious control on the part of the patient. When the body is thoroughly relaxed, the patient can go further through the nervous and mental phases of relaxation.* At the same time he affirms and attempts to realize in full consciousness the supporting power of the divine Life, 'in which we live and move and have our being'. To do this he will use any words or ideas that can make the experience real to himself. This phase is, if one likes to term it so, an autosuggestion of the immediacy and the abundance of healing 'grace', and it can act as balm to tired mind, overstrained feelings and exhausted nerves.

When the technique is understood and used with simplicity it may be surprisingly effective. Deep relaxation in itself allows the body to recuperate. The quieting of the mind and of the feelings permits synchronization of the psychic field with a more rhythmic flow of the vital energies in the body. When the vital and the psychic fields are aligned and quietened, an opening of the inner consciousness towards the all-enveloping Life can take place, which then allows that Life to flow freely into the whole nature, working its own deep healing and refreshment.

The above description is cursory, but many practitioners of varying schools who use the above or similar techniques of conscious relaxation, plus the affirmation of the healing power of the indwelling Life, agree upon its deep restorative effect.

* See 'The New Way to Relax', by Karen Roon. World's Work Publishers. Also 'You Must Relax', Jacobson. McGraw-Hill.

CHAPTER VI

THOUGHT POWER: A NATURAL ENERGY

So often we try to take from people the burdens they alone can
carry effectively and creatively, before their work is done ...
  If more invalids could be led to realize that their weakness
is no excuse for bad manners and for behaving like a spoilt
child, many might emerge more mature than before they were
ill and be better adjusted to life. But being ill alone will not
bring the capacity to rise above it and turn even that to good
account. And the attitude of doctors, nurses and visiting clergy,
is of fundamental importance in evoking this constructive
attitude in their patients.

'Religion and Psychology', *A. Graham Ikin*

AT this point it seems wise to draw together certain threads
that have run somewhat at random through this book, and
to show their connection and underlying implications. Much that
has been said is not new; much would be fully accepted by en-
lightened medical and psychological practitioners; much would
be fully supported by priests and lay workers who deal with
chronic illness in their daily work. But certain fundamental concepts have been touched upon which are too frequently overlooked, doubted, ignored and even denied—and further stress may
usefully be laid upon these. In particular there is need to make
very clear to the modern mind the ancient teaching regarding the
formative power of thought.

The universe itself is said in the Hindu scriptures to come into
being by the action of a formative power, termed *mahat*, a principle in nature which underlies the creation of all forms. Mahat is
in the universe what manas, or mind, is in the individual. The
Taitiriyopanishad states: 'Mind is Brahm. From mind indeed ...
these creatures have their birth. By mind, when born, they live;
to mind they go, they pass away'. (Part III) And the *Aitareyo-
panishad* begins: 'The SELF indeed alone, was verily in the beginning ... He had the thought: Now let me worlds evolve'. Plato,
looking at the universe as it were from within outwards, pictures
the Demiurge, the Creative Principle, as 'taking thought' and

building a universe that conformed to reason (*Timaeus*, 29 D-30c). Pythagoras taught that God geometrizes, and Plato considered that the Formative Principle expressed itself through reason and logic, and hence was able to bring a certain coherence out of Chaos. The world, he said, is shaped by pure reason (nous) which also provides the archetypal patterns for all forms.*

This is of course true of human creative activity—the plan or pattern comes first and after that, directed action. Emotion can involve a momentary unity, a creative urge, but for the co-ordination of conscious feeling with action some kind of mental patterning is essential.

This may seem to have little to do with healing, but it is only as we measure thought by its infinite capacity for creation that we can understand its use and effect in this field.

The formative power of thought and its capacity to build an interior model or pattern, which hands and body can then bring into physical manifestation, is nothing new. Every artist, architect, inventor or strategist is familiar with the technique. What is needed in healing is a clear realization that the mind directs forces in the unseen worlds which immediately affect the body. Thought and emotion are forces that modify, for better or for worse, the subtle psychic currents which affect the life of the physical form.

In practice, thought and emotion are normally inseparable, though they can be separated, just as one can distinguish and discuss form and colour in a picture where they exist together. Thought represents the stable, shaping element, whereas emotion is the fluid, labile energy which works in and through the thought structure. If the thought is steady, the emotional currents play a secondary part, and flow in the channels prepared for them by thought. If, on the other hand, the thinking is chaotic or blurred, and the emotions riotous, the thought structure becomes distorted and broken by torrential streams of feeling. If the thought patterns are rigid, the mind tends to be obsessional, or at any rate prejudiced and biased. If the emotions are rampant, clear sense of direction is lost. But where the thought is at once pliable and

* Modern research in biology is leading to the acceptance of the idea that some sort of psychic pattern or 'organizer' must exist to control such changes as that of the grub to the butterfly. See 'Matter, Mind and Man', E. W. Sinnott, published by Harper. Chapters IV, V, VII, etc. Also 'The Human Heritage', by Sir Heneage Ogilvie, K.B.E., LL.D., F.R.C.S., in *The Lancet*, July 6, 1957.

resilient, existing in clear patterns and purpose, feeling can flow freely and strongly through such patterning.

Along with the idea of the formative power of thought, then, we need to associate the fact that just as there is physical energy of various types, so also psychic energy varies in its mental and emotional effects. Some thought and emotional patterns are constructive, others destructive, to physical health. Gloom, bitterness, excessive criticism, tend to restrict or distort the nervous activities and exhaust reserves of physical energy. Clear, positive ideas, however, associated with an inner sense of quietude and of the goodness of things, tend to release energy in the body and bring about health. This applies not only to individuals but also to the community as a whole, for the community consists of individuals, all thinking and feeling for themselves, but pouring the fruits of their mental activity into the collective pool.

Something of this is now widely recognized by scientific investigators who have been exploring in many directions the problems of thought and feeling, both in the social sphere and, more recently, in their relation to nervous activity. The accumulated material has become so extensive as to justify the formation of a new branch of medicine, the psycho-somatic, which we have already mentioned. Among other instruments invented to further this study is the electro-encephalograph: this registers the reactions of nerve impulses in the brain as they are influenced by thought and feeling. The apparatus demonstrates not only the modification of the brain cells and their activity due to disease and tissue deterioration, but also variations of pattern in nerve reactions which are induced by different types of feeling and thinking in perfectly normal brain cells.* Reports issued by various groups which are now appearing in journals all over the world, show the interest roused by such experiments, and all confirm the fact that harsh, unco-ordinated reactions in the psyche bring about disorder and fatigue of brain tissue, while confidence and optimism produce more harmonious and less exhausting impulses.

As is now well known, Dr J. B. Rhine has carried the experimental study of thought as a natural energy even further, and devised a method to demonstrate the effect of concentrated thought upon the movement of inanimate objects.† Dr Rhine used

---

* See 'The Living Brain', Grey Walter. Duckworth.
† See 'The New Frontiers of the Mind', J. B. Rhine. Pelican.

dice, mechanically thrown at random, which during their fall are subjected to the concentrated thought of the experimenter, who visualizes them powerfully as falling in a given pattern, say double threes. Thousands of repeated experiments have shown that the thought of the operator does affect the fall of the physical objects, the results being definitely above the known mathematical laws of chance. All possible explanations other than the claimed result have been fully allowed for, and eliminated by technical apparatus in modern laboratory fashion. Accepted scientific methods are used for checking and rechecking. In other words, the power of thought to affect the action of physical matter is now an established scientific fact, subject to test by laboratory techniques. Rhine calls the power which affects the dice *psychokinetic energy*, and he insists that it is a natural energy, not yet recognized by orthodox science, except as it has been proved to exist in the laboratories of the parapsychologists. The dice are held to be inert matter, with no mental background or associations, so the theory is that the operator's psychokinetic energy directly influences their physical movements.

In the teachings of the Ancient Wisdom, thought is said to be analogous in nature to electricity, and this may help in studying its effects upon physical matter, and also its influence between mind and mind. The idea of thought as electric is reflected in common phrases. One switches one's thought off and on, if one has learned how to do so; one charges oneself with an idea; the mind is illumined by a particular thought, and so on, all reflecting intuitively the similarity of the action of thought to that of electrical energy. The effect of 'currents of thought' upon individuals is well known, as in advertising, and in changing fashions of thought and manners.

If Rhine's experiments are sound—and so far the most determined attack from skilled scientists has been unable to break them down—then thought acts at its own level, and can affect both objects and persons from that level. When human beings send a thought from mind to mind, the phenomenon is called telepathy. Here again Dr Rhine has made sustained experiments, and those interested are referred to his writings. In the ancient teachings the phenomena associated with one mind influencing another are likened to the processes of induction and resonance in electrical apparatus. In mental healing, for example, the practitioner has a strong realization of the healing power of Life. This healing Life is projected around the patient by thought and the will to heal. The patient may be either present or absent, for in this respect thought does not seem to be conditioned by distance. If the patient is in tune with the healer, he receives the flow of Life sent by the healer, is bathed in it, and consciously or unconsciously accepts it, making it his own. In healing work this is as commonplace a phenomenon as it is for a properly constructed electrical apparatus to influence another without physical contact, if there is the right adjustment between them. The phenomena of wireless and television depend upon the working of such a relationship through what we term 'properly tuned in' physical apparatus. Under suitable conditions an electrical current is induced in the receiving instrument without direct contact with the sending mechanism. The parallel to mental healing is extremely close, and repays study.

It is, of course, not only healers who broadcast thought, but everyone everywhere and all the time. Few people have strong, independent or trained minds, and so the thought world is full of drifting, half-shaped energies, of very low potency. But for better or for worse, these play upon us all the time—spreading doubt, misery, unkind ideas of others, or communicating a certain goodwill, optimism, friendliness, which people feel at given times as oppressive or helpful, as the case may be.

We can then sum up the position as it has been stated in the olden days, and as it is now being demonstrated in modern research laboratories. *Thought is a specific force in nature. In the human individual, thought continually brings about changes in the physical body. Personal thought also continually plays upon and influences one's associates and one's environment.*

Do those who are attempting to heal others in both orthodox and unorthodox ways use this force constructively and to its fullest extent for the purposes of healing?

We have in fairness to admit that certain unorthodox groups have been mainly responsible for awakening the western mind to a conscious recognition that the power of thought can bring about healthier conditions in the physical body. We owe much to the impact of Christian Science and to the Unity Movement, with their myriad derivative groups, because these have demonstrated clearly that much human thinking is negative and destructive in effect, failing altogether to release life freely in either mind or body. But orthodox practitioners, on the whole, have discredited such movements because extravagant claims are made on their behalf, and also because serious illness has frequently failed to have adequate attention under their practitioners.

In the same way, the power of positive suggestion—brought into the limelight by Coué, Bernheim and others—is not as a rule seriously considered nor used consciously as part of routine treatments. In medical schools the student will be advised to give his dose with the statement, 'This is just what you need', or 'This will do you good', but no great emphasis is maintained upon the point. Certain doctors have innately a good encouraging presence, evoking confidence and a positive reaction to their suggestions and treatment. These may be pointed out for admiration, but a conscious study or exposition of the interaction between the mind of the doctor and that of his patient is usually lacking in medical circles. Examples of successful treatments by practitioners who have developed an habitually constructive psychological approach are rarely sought out, and if noted at all in medical training are not sufficiently understood.

This fact has not escaped the eyes of modern investigators. Professor Sorokin* secured the co-operation of certain nurses and attendants in a psychiatric ward of Harvard Hospital. At his instigation, and as an experiment, the staff was induced to use a special technique of kindly sympathy and to encourage the patients to adopt a more optimistic view of life. It was not that the staff had been unkind or indifferent before: they had been thoroughly competent and professional. But when a gentler, more sympathetic and generally more encouraging approach was used, it had immediate beneficial effect upon a significant number of those included in the experiment.

This is to be expected—but its deep significance is still unrecognized. The mechanistic age is with us, and 'suitable' drugs, 'observational experiments' and pattern formations are more considered than the effect of one mind upon another. Yet the fact

---

* See 'Forms and Techniques of Altruistic and Spiritual Growth', Beacon Press, Boston. Edited by P. A. Sorokin; Harvard Research Centre of Creative Altruism.

remains that the right use of suggestion does affect the flow of vital energy, or assist in changing a 'pattern formation', by giving the patient a sense of the existence of positive possibilities, and encouraging him to hope and work for his own improvement.*

It is because the effect of mind upon mind is at present rather overshadowed by laboratory tests, routine diagnoses, X-ray examinations and the like, that the importance of the psychological interplay between healer and patient is here so strongly emphasized. Factual, business-like laboratory investigations may be exact, and give precise information and hence confidence to the practitioner. But however well such information is used, it needs to be supplemented by insight and by the personal understanding and encouragement of the old family-doctor relationship. Just as no amount of laboratory tests can take the place of diagnostic insight, so also no tonic is as fundamentally effective as the sense of being understood and encouraged by a person in whose judgment the patient has real confidence.

Let it be perfectly clear that no reasonable person wishes doctors or nurses to promise the impossible. That has grave disadvantages, and is one of the major criticisms of unorthodox healers, who—while they give positive suggestion—frequently ignore the seriousness of some cases that come to them. But it is the fact that the right use of positive thought directly affects the flow of vital energy in a patient and encourages him to hope for, · indeed to expect, improvement, and so makes that improvement more possible. This takes place because such positive thinking, when natural and based upon a reasonable expectation, is itself creative, and stimulates mental and emotional currents which in turn directly impinge on the vital activities of the body, and set this working on curative lines.† The work mentioned above, in which encephalograms were taken of patients thinking frightened thoughts, and again when more pleasant conditions of the psyche were induced, shows that the rhythm of nervous activity immediately changes when hopeful or pleasing states of mind are induced.

* The best psychological treatment always takes this attitude, but too often the technique of the particular school to which a psychologist belongs dominates the treatment. The successful psychological practitioner is usually one whose personal effect upon the patient is of far greater significance than his technique. See Chapter V.

† See 'Some Unrecognized Factors in Medicine', Chapter III, for details. Also Chapter V of this book, under 'Autosuggestion', page 41.

There is a further point in regard to prognosis and the expectation of improvement. In these days, when so much exact information is at the disposal of the intelligent practitioner, it is not surprising if he tends to accept averages as the basis of his expectation in regard to the possibility or degree of the patient's recovery. Yet the wise physician or surgeon will always allow for the exception, and can easily give just the right psychological impulse that will enable the exceptional cure to take place. The exact truth may be told the patient, if with that information there is also given the further knowledge that nature has immense reserves, and can substitute for loss, as well as re-adjust and attune the body to special needs, provided the mind is healthily alert, and the emotions reasonably peaceful or constructively occupied. The expectation of even slight improvement is creative in effect.

It may seem to be asking too much that the doctor, nurse or healer should always be—within reason—optimistic and suitably encouraging. But such an attitude is capable of cultivation. It is indeed an axiom of many schools of thought, both ancient and modern, that conscious introspection and growth in self-awareness can lead to quieter, more constructive and more potent use of thought and of emotion.* And in these days the constructive use of thought for healing purposes is widely and deeply needed. The counters of multiple stores are littered with cheap, highly advertised drugs for inducing sleep or relieving pain; a surgical operation is looked upon quite as a matter of course in a normal life; if there is an epidemic of influenza one is almost expected to be ill and is thought to be 'lucky' to escape it. Yet health is normal: disease is aberrant. As thoughtful people, let us turn once more to the fundamental powers latent in each one of us, and instead of assuming disease to be inevitable, and searching for antidotes, begin to rediscover and use appropriately the immense potency of the Life within, with its deep cleansing and regenerative power. Thought is a force in nature: it is time we learned to use that force consciously and creatively.

A few words may also be said about the help that could be— and frequently is—given through the association of a spiritual centre, such as an oratory or chapel, with special hospitals. While every hospital recognizes the need for physical cleanliness, not

* See 'Some Unrecognized Factors in Medicine', Chapter V, under *Special Techniques*.

many consciously recognize the need for psychic clarity and disinfection. Yet hospitals where sacramental aids are used are often remarkable for the peaceful and healing atmosphere that is present. In times to come, when the inner side of disease and of healing is better understood, it should be possible for groups of people living in the neighbourhood of institutions of healing, mental homes, and so on, to be trained to keep active a centre for prayer and meditation in connection with each institution. The technique would have to be studied, and personnel would need to be specially selected. Thought and aspiration are the operative factors in such activities, and they could be directed to maintaining a positive psychic cleanliness, and a constructive mental atmosphere, throughout such institutions, as well as to sustaining for the patients both hope, and contact with the inner healing life.

There is in such work a splendid opportunity for collaboration with the unseen forces in nature, especially with those angels which are associated with healing and the relief of pain and with the significant transitions of consciousness that are known as birth and death.

The rationale of such work will be discussed in a later chapter, but it is appropriate here to mention these possibilities. Once it is recognized that thought is a creative energy, which it is—to some extent at least—within man's power to evoke and direct, the value of groups that are capable of working in collaboration with the unseen forces of nature at the mental and even spiritual levels, must sooner or later be fully acknowledged.

CHAPTER VII

VARIOUS UNORTHODOX TREATMENTS AND METHODS OF DIAGNOSIS

There are more things in Heaven and Earth, Horatio,
Than are dreamt of in your philosophy.

'Hamlet', *Shakespeare*

THE LAYING ON OF HANDS
AND VITAL MAGNETIC TREATMENT

MANY methods of treatment are covered by the term 'the laying on of hands', but all involve the transference of vital and possibly spiritual energies by and through the practitioner to the patient by means of the hands, the breath, or his mere presence. This transfer may sometimes take place without the practitioner being aware of what he is doing; this is the case with many doctors whose presence seems to convey healing power. It is by no means always a phenomenon to be explained on psychological grounds, for it frequently involves a considerable channelling of physical vitality through the doctor to the patient, although neither is clearly conscious of what is happening. Sometimes such transfers occur merely because one person has an excess of vital energy which he distributes automatically without conscious direction or design.

In deliberate healing of this type various sources of energy may be drawn upon. The healer may use the forces of his own personality, adding to them perhaps by auto-suggestion and thereby canalizing the latent but readily available vitality of the atmosphere.* One type of healer draws upon the vitality of persons who may be near, thus merely acting as a means of conveying the vitality of a group to his patient. Another type will have contacts with healing angels or devas who readily co-operate in such work, but of whom the healer may be entirely unaware. Any strong magnetic healer in all probability has attendants in the unseen worlds, who are more likely to be devic than human.† Many healers who regard

* See Chapter IV, pp. 23-25 and 50
† See Chapter VIII, 'Healing Angels'.

themselves as being guided by important persons 'on the other side' may really be using their own semi-conscious and intuitive diagnostic faculties reinforced by help from a strong thought-form and its ensouling devic entity.*

In all cases where the healer does not become depleted he is acting as a channel for natural vital energy, drawn from one source or another. For certain temperaments it is easier to draw upon the almost unlimited supply of such vitality if the healer envisages this as emanating from a source outside himself, and as being given 'through' him, directed by some kind of unseen guide. A healer of another type will prefer to put himself consciously under the direction of his own highest consciousness and specialize the needed vital force by means of deep breathing and by opening himself deliberately to the healing currents at various levels. Whether consciously or unconsciously, he will draw upon the level that is appropriate to the case or which he is accustomed to use.

This leads to a consideration of the very different types of healers who employ some form of 'the laying on of hands'. There are those of a vigorous physical type, often extremely successful with cases of congestion or inertia, who draw upon the uprising earth forces, mixed with psychic energy of a rather strong, heavy quality, often perfectly clean and pure, but of a slower vibratory rate than others. They may be sincere, dedicated people, but they are using, nevertheless, vital energies connected with the ordinary growth processes in nature, and while their treatment is beneficial to some people, it is not suitable for all types of patients.

Others draw from subtler vital levels, those associated specifically with human thought and feeling. The energy derived from these is not necessarily to be considered as more spiritual either in source or in effect; all nature is a manifestation of the divine life. But the treatment has a somewhat gentler quality and hence may be more or less useful according to the type of case. The distinction may be said to be one of wave-length, like the difference between treatments with infra-red and ultra-violet radiations.

Yet other healers claim that they rely purely upon 'spiritual' sources of energy, and use nothing so earthly as human vitality or magnetism. But in all cases where the physical vital energy of the patient is directly enhanced, there must be some flow of force at the physical level between healer and subject, and in many

* See pp. 58, 66, 67 and 79.

treatments termed spiritual or mental, a transfer of such physical vitality does certainly take place.

It is also true that healers working effectively at the mental and spiritual levels likewise induce an increased flow of physical vitality in the patient. In these cases the physical improvement takes place as a secondary result incidental to some interior re-adjustment. The real trouble has been adequately dealt with at its own level and release from interior maladjustment or conflict induces a freer flow of energy in the physical body.

Not unnaturally, an alteration in the psyche by such interior methods is more likely to bring about real and lasting cure, that is a deeper re-adjustment to life, than treatments aimed at physical health alone, and therefore given only at the physical level. Many of those engaged in giving treatments for improving physical vitality recognize this and try to work at the various higher levels concurrently.

VITAL MAGNETIC HEALING

The term vital magnetic healing is employed to describe the conscious use of vital energy, drawn from almost any source, which is conveyed to the patient largely through the healer's hands. Ever since the time of Mesmer, who was not such a charla-tan as he is often painted, many practitioners in the West have used this method to relieve local congestion, to increase the flow of nervous energy, and to relax and revivify patients suffering from shock or exhaustion. The practice is rarely intelligently understood, and in the hands of the ignorant may savour of superstitious 'magic'; claims are frequently made for it which far exceed its real value.

It has, however, a well developed technique, the right and left hands acting as poles for the discharge of vitality, and certain 'passes' being used for the direction of this energy to relieve congestion or to feed depleted areas, etc.*

All that has been said about the various sources from which vital energy can be drawn for the laying on of hands applies to this method, as does also the description of the different types of healers. It is frequently employed by 'spirit healers', working 'under control', and is then sometimes described as 'power' from

* See 'Vital Magnetic Healing' by A. Gardner, Theosophical Publishing House.

the loftiest levels of existence. At worst, it may become a superstitious act for which vast and ill-founded claims have been made.
At best, as a conscious technique which can be deliberately
trained, critically examined and improved, it may be viewed as a
controlled method of transferring energy from a healer to a
patient, without detriment to the healer and with considerable
benefit to suitable patients.

Although many who use it would not agree, vital magnetic
healing is essentially a physical treatment affecting the body somewhat as do massage and other stimulating treatments that come
under the head of physiotherapy. If the one who gives massage
happens also to be a healer of the vital magnetic type—and many
masseurs are—a considerable flow of subtle healing energy is
likely to be transferred to the patient during the treatment. A
masseur who understands this aspect of his work is often singularly successful with special types of nervous disorder, and, even
when the vital stimulation or soothing is performed unconsciously,
a masseur who possesses this faculty stands out from others as
having 'unusually good hands for such work'.

In common with all other purely physical treatments, the effect
of magnetic healing may easily be nullified by psychological re-
gression, and since its action is more subtle than that of dense
physical medicaments, the results it produces have even less power
than the latter to resist the effects of psychological changes in the
patient.

It should be understood that magnetic healing does not act
directly on the tissues of the nervous system, but induces changes
in the dense physical body by altering the flow of vitality at the
subtle etheric levels. Hence arises its particular value in the treatment of shock; for post-operative conditions, including delayed
anaesthetic poisoning; in convalescence from all diseases;
and as an important aid in the readjustment of physiological
dysfunction.

On the other hand, it is definitely unsuitable in the treatment
of hysterics, and is very readily misused by patients who demand a great deal of attention. It is obviously useless for those
who demand a quick, cheap cure, involving no effort on their
part. Headache, neuralgia, various forms of cramp, often yield
readily *in suitable cases*; but where these symptoms are the outcome of some deep-seated trouble, such as organic disease, they

will reappear quickly after magnetic treatment, and other methods must be used to bring about a permanent cure.

Some misunderstanding in regard to all methods involving 'the laying on of hands' arises in part because they are so often associated with religious practices, orthodox or unorthodox. Such association with religious dogmatism, and the unwillingness on the part of some practitioners to submit results to impartial investigation, should not blind students to the empirical evidence that vital energy can be, and often is, transmitted from one person to another and, in suitable cases, with great benefit. Healers who use a conscious technique, such as is here termed vital magnetic healing, would wish for further investigations and a wider use of the possibilities of such treatment as a substitute for tranquilizing and stimulating drugs. It is indeed a well established fact that, whether the treatment is given by a healer full of dense earthy vitality, or sustained and infused by the subtlest of spiritual forces working down to the physical level from within, the essential facts are the same: in such treatments, a transference of vital force takes place through the healer to the patient whereby the physical body of the patient may benefit very considerably.

MENTAL AND ABSENT TREATMENTS

Mental and absent treatments depend upon telepathic rapport; hence it is essential that the minds of healer and patient should be to some degree in harmony. Once it is recognized that the mental world, although much more subtle than the physical, appears to have certain characteristics similar to physical matter, with its own vibratory rates, its own vital energies, as well as mental forms and structures, the comprehension of mental healing on its technical side will be much simplified.

The analogy of sound-resonance suggests itself. When a singer sings a certain note, nearby objects capable of vibrating at the same frequency will tend to oscillate in sympathy and thus sound the same note. In the case of inert objects the response soon stops when the singer ceases to sound that particular note; but in a living being the effect may linger for a considerable time in the mind of the hearer, and if the effect has been the release of healing vitality, this can then be sustained by the patient's own mental images.

In this way, when a healer directs a strong thought towards a patient or a friend in trouble, the other person—if he has it in him to respond—may react in harmony with the healing thought, often with startling results. But the healer's thought, to be effective, must be based both on a clear realization that the other person is in difficulties, and on a sincere desire to help. The healer needs also to appreciate that the illness as manifested may reflect much deeper conditions, and in fact may be a beneficial safety-valve for these. To attempt to direct a thought, let us say, towards curing an attack of insomnia, may be to treat a superficial symptom while leaving untouched some profound psychological disturbance which is at the root of the trouble, and while such treatment may be temporarily successful it is not likely to get to the fundamental cause.

The absence of the patient, and his possible unawareness of the moment when the healing effort is made, may be a positive advantage because, being unconscious of what is happening, he is neither resistant nor over-anxious to be helpful and responsive. Both these attitudes create etheric tension and frequently inhibit the action of what would otherwise have been beneficial influences. In this connection it is interesting that laboratory experiments with extra-sensory perception have shown that ideas lying on the fringe of the sender's consciousness often register with the recipient more clearly and truly than those upon which the sender's attention has been fully centred. Relaxation of the mind—as we have so frequently observed—eases etheric tension and so *permits* phenomena to occur in a less obstructed field. This principle is closely applicable to mental healing. Directed helpful thought sent towards a friend, even if one is unaware that he or she is ill and in need of it, may do more good than a later deliberate attempt to heal. In such a case some accident of synchronicity, as it were, allows the flow of healing power to take place effectively. The contrary, however, is at times also true—that deliberately directed effort and conscious reception can be surprisingly successful. Much depends upon the singleness of mind, the faith and the expectancy of both parties.

As is the case in all other methods of healing, a dedicated worker can call upon help from agencies in the unseen worlds. Strong belief in the power of thought, or in the efficacy of prayer, brings unseen help to those who need it, and an evocation of the healing power of a saint, or of the Christ, will augment the effectiveness of the treatment, since such an evocation establishes contact with subtle and powerful healing agencies.

In all attempts to understand the principles involved in the foregoing concepts it is necessary to hold in mind the fact that each thought has a natural elemental power of its own—is, in fact, a mental energy, shaped well or indifferently for its purpose as the case may be. It persists in accordance with the clarity, strength, and sustenance given to it by its creator. It may also be directed and sustained by various orders of nature spirits, angels, and healing powers, which are associated with ritual groups or are summoned by the thought of a competent healer. The sending of a healing thought to a friend or patient is not quite so simple a thing as is commonly supposed. It was mentioned above that tension at any level can stiffen the patient's or the healer's nervous reactions, to the disadvantage of the treatment, but on the other hand, the auto-suggestive quality of strong faith undoubtedly increases effectiveness.

Cases are on record where a devoted relative has held steadily the thought of healing around one who was critically ill, and the patient, although unaware at the time that help was being invoked on his behalf, has later described the healing and protective influences he has felt surrounding him during the major crisis of his illness.

There are also many authentic cases of what appear to be visits in the sleep state on the part of friends to those who were ill. In these, the friend or healer projects himself in thought towards the patient and gives such help as is possible, focussing a stream of gentle healing energy on the centre of disorder, or soothing severe pain by what appears to be a form of vital magnetic energy. It is impossible to determine in such cases whether the healer's psyche actually travels to the patient when the healer is asleep, or whether a strong thought-form is sent by the healer, charged with intention so that healing vitality streams through the projected image. In either case it is the mind and the will of the healer that are operative and produce the resultant healing experience.

Thought being a powerful energy, it is evident that a self-opinionated healer who has a fixed idea about his patient, can actually do harm by concentrating too much upon a particular organ, when the disease of that part of the body may be but secondary to more profound disturbances; over-emphasis on that part might then be detrimental to the general healing processes. At the other extreme, there is the vague healer who desires to be helpful but is unable to concentrate sufficiently to do more than 'wish that something might be done'. Cases have been reported where the first type, being really well-informed, has been singularly successful in healing a specific trouble, but a more general method—where, as in Christian Science, the healing power of the Divine Mind is affirmed, with no reference whatever to any specific disease—is usually more likely to be beneficial.

When a known physical disease is being treated, a moderate view between these two extremes might be expressed thus: 'May this patient receive what is needed for his recovery and may his whole being, body and soul, be bathed in healing life'.

Mental healing is conditioned as to its effects by all the factors that have been enumerated in relation to other subtle methods. At its best, it can be almost miraculously effective, carrying a serious case through a crisis, restoring morale, bringing a sense of reserve strength or a peace that fosters rapid physical recovery. At its worst, it may prove meddlesome, introducing cross-currents and unnecessary stresses. In the opinion of the writers it should never be employed in cases where there is any personal antagonism to the healer, or resistance to unorthodox methods of healing.*

PSYCHIC DIAGNOSIS AND RADIAESTHESIA

The use of psychic powers for the diagnosis of disease is as old as history, and in ancient times was often officially connected with temples where specially trained, and often very skilled, priests or priestesses, engaged in the study and treatment of disease, used psychic diagnosis, medicinal remedies, and surgery according to their special gifts, training and tradition.

Nowadays, a clairvoyant or psychometrist, who consciously directs his own activities and has developed the faculty of diagnosing physical diseases, can often give a most accurate analysis of the physical conditions in a patient's body, such as pointing out lesions in the spine, dysfunction in deeply embedded organs, states of exhaustion in nerve-centres, and so on. Some of these psychics

* See also Chapter V, under 'Suggestion'; and Chapter VIII, 'Healing Groups'.

derive benefit from an added training along medical lines; others are aided by a developed intuitive sense of where to look for the focus of trouble and how to interpret the symptoms.

In order to appraise the value of this type of work it is necessary to review very briefly the modern methods of physical diagnosis. It is not infrequently claimed that current scientific techniques for examining and testing the condition and functioning of the physical body have raised medical diagnosis to the level of an exact science. Against this assumption stands the fact that the physical body is an elaborately compounded organism whose parts are inter-related in such a complicated fashion, that even to-day much of its mechanism remains obscure or incompletely understood. It is not surprising, therefore, that really great clinicians when faced with an unusually puzzling case, fall back upon the human intuition as the surest guide.* The efficient family doctor uses his intuition continually, although when in doubt he will certainly avail himself of laboratory tests. It remains true, then, that the 'direct interior perception' of an intuitive individual can be as effective and trustworthy as delicate scientific apparatus and that it is, moreover, usually required for an accurate interpretation of the scientific findings. There are not a few good physicians and surgeons whose unconscious extra-sensory perceptions are the cause and basis of their distinction, though in such cases this is usually ascribed to what is called clinical sense, or insight.

Clairvoyant Diagnosis. With this background we come to the discussion of diagnosis by psychic means only. This may be studied under two headings: that of clairvoyance and that of psychometric ability. The difference between the two is comparable to the difference between the visual sense and the sense of touch. There is also a generalized psychic capacity which does not actually fall within the scope of either of these two categories.

Clairvoyants with a technical knowledge of anatomy and physiology are rare, but there are many psychics with varying capacities for diagnosis, which they employ either consciously or 'under control'.† Their methods vary from trance—with a presumed medical 'guide'—to conscious use of the hands over the body of their patients, 'feeling' the congested or inflamed areas

* See 'Some Unrecognized Factors in Medicine', Chapter V.
† See pp. 66 and 67.

and intuitively guessing or possibly psychometrizing the origin and nature of the disorder. When such guesses derive from a clear extra-sensory contact, and are clarified by reliable intuitive insight, the diagnosis can be amazingly accurate. Mediums working 'under control' vary enormously in their capacities, and the larger claims commonly made are rarely tested or capable of substantiation. Nevertheless the public is interested in this method and at times has a childlike faith in it. Such methods should, however, be carefully distinguished from those which involve direct seeing, a capacity to look, more or less clearly, within the physical body of the patient to the point where the disorder is situated, and to describe the exact position of an infection, a growth, or a strained muscle.

Unlike the psychometrist, the clairvoyant does not touch the patient, but carefully observes the conditions existing both in the dense physical and in the etheric bodies. For clairvoyance, literally 'clear seeing', is the power to bring through, into the ordinary waking consciousness of the physical brain, impressions received in terms of the visual sense, which enable the percipient clearly to envisage and so to describe what is taking place either within the dense physical body or in its etheric counterpart. All such vision is a capacity or function of the personality and is not necessarily synonymous with spiritual illumination. Like the clinical sense of the doctor, it is inevitably tinged with some degree of the seer's own psychological make-up. Yet, because the psychic can actually observe phenomena hidden to ordinary sight, extra-sensory perception can and does help to track down subtle disorders. Through the power of the observer to look directly at deeply hidden parts of the body, he is often able to see the cause of a condition which would otherwise remain obscure, or which might require an exploratory operation merely for diagnosis.

A clairvoyant of such skill and training that he can focus his vision at the etheric level with precision and direct it to any area he wishes to observe, is obviously of great value in medical and surgical work, but they are rare. Nevertheless experiments with individual clairvoyants of this order have been, and are now being, made in various countries, with the co-operation of reliable physicians, scientifically critical but open-minded, who value such capacities and are prepared to take advantage of them in problem cases. In these experiments, clairvoyant diagnoses are methodically checked and verified by X-ray photography, while surgical treatment has often confirmed the findings.

Many healers at the outset of their work possess a vague power to sense conditions of health and disease but require some suggestion either from the patient or from an outside source to crystallize their impressions into definite form. They may also become confused or etherically fatigued. Untrained psychics of this type, while able at times to illumine patients and friends by an inexplicable flash of penetration, find that at other times their translation or interpretation of inner impressions falls very wide of the mark.

Psychics of this type usually work more through the feelings than the mind; hence their sensitivity is involuntary and functions through the sympathetic nervous system, and the solar plexus is the usual avenue through which diagnostic impressions are conveyed and received in the consciousness. They are seldom clairvoyant (though they commonly say they 'see' a special condition or can 'sense' a diseased organ), nor do they possess conscious psychometric capacity. The disadvantage of work of this kind is that it is bound to be of the hit or miss order and consequently it may—with the best of intentions—do a great deal of harm by confusing or misleading those concerned.

Psychometry may be defined as an increased power of sensing by touch. It can be developed from the sensitivity described above, or it may exist spontaneously as a special faculty. Once this faculty has become established as a definite 'sense', etheric or physical contact with the patient, or with some object he has handled, is all that is needed. This appears to put the psychic in touch with the conditions which exist within the physical and etheric bodies of the patient, which are then interpreted with greater or less accuracy according to the psychic's skill.

Methods of making contact depend upon the variety and quality of the psychometrist's capacity and experience. One will prefer simply to hold the hand of the patient; another will ask for some article with which the latter has been in close contact; a third will run his hands over the patient's body.

In the study of all such extra-sensory methods of diagnosis, the existence of the vital or etheric emanations around the patient needs constantly to be borne in mind, as well as the reality of the psychic field within which his personal consciousness is active.

Both the vital emanations and the habitual mental and emotional activities of any individual are more or less visible or tangible to a person trained in extra-sensory perception. For any one given case the variation in reports from a series of percipients will depend first upon their innate extra-sensory capacity, and then upon training, impersonality, and the skill they have developed in its use. The psychometrist possesses extra-sensory touch, the clairvoyant extra-sensory sight; but the range of capacity in each case will vary *with the result that diagnoses are by no means infallible, and not infrequently lack discrimination.*

Radiaesthesia is, in effect, a form of psychometry, aided by mechanical apparatus. This is not always recognized, but the fact remains that it is so. The mechanism used may be a simple divining rod, a pendulum, a complicated Abrams 'box', or one of the machines used for such work under the modern title 'radiaesthesia' or 'radionics'.

In the view of the writers, *all* such techniques are based upon certain underlying principles and can therefore be grouped together for study. So far as diagnosis is concerned these principles can best be understood by comparing them with the modern electro-cardiogram. This is a purely physical machine which uses ordinary electric currents to create a magnetic field. The latter is then used to amplify, and hence detect and register, the minute electric currents produced by the action of various parts of the heart. It is the *amplification* of the minute impulses which enables them to be detected and recorded.

It is now admitted by those who use the various types of diagnostic machines associated with radiaesthesia that for successful work it is necessary to have present a human operator of a special type. It is also well known that some operators are more proficient than others, while in the case of certain people the machine will not work at all. This leads to the following analysis of the process as now in general use in many countries.

The patient is required to provide a spot of blood or saliva, or a letter. This acts as a key-factor, a link, relating the patient to the operator through the mechanism of the machine into which it is inserted. The operator, who must possess either conscious or unconscious extra-sensory perception (a faculty more prevalent than many would think), in the process of operating the machine subjectively psychometrises the vital emanations of the given specimen. This subjective psychometry is in turn capable of creating sufficiently strong unconscious muscular movements to produce oscillation of a pendulum, or to alter etheric tension in the operator, so that the indicator in the instrument is affected.

It is thus the unconscious extra-sensory perception of the operator, picking up the psychic overtones of the specimen, and using the machine as a focus, which affects the indicators in positive or negative fashion. This process is as unrelated to the *conscious* mind of the operator as is the movement of a water-diviner's rod.*

Thus the mechanism used in these methods of diagnosis, whether it be a pendulum, a divining rod passed over the body, a complicated box of dials, or a photographic apparatus, is merely a means for the precise externalization of the unconscious extra-sensory perceptions of the operator, *whether these are accurate or not*. The claim hitherto made that these machines are 'a purely physical and scientific means' of diagnosis and treatment, cannot be substantiated under the present terms of scientific knowledge. That they exemplify the working of certain laws of nature, still largely obscure or unrecognized, is certainly true. But no good will be done either to medical or to psychic research by denying or ignoring the psychic and psychological factors involved in their use.** It should be recognised, too, that the 'psychic camera', which photographs a diseased liver or other organ, is really producing on the plate or film a psychic 'extra' of the operator's own thought-form—a by no means unfamiliar phenomenon in psychical research.†

Hence it follows that the accuracy or inaccuracy of diagnosis by radiaesthesia will depend upon all the usual factors involved in psychic and in medical work—experience, impersonality, and the conscious or unconscious psychic capacities of the operator. Favourable and unfavourable psychic conditions, including the resistance or sympathy or expectation of the patient, as well as the clarity or complexity of the case, must all be included among the modifying factors.

* See 'Physics of the Divining Rod', Maby and Franklin. Bell & Sons, 1939, London.

**Satisfactory results can be obtained without any specimen in the machine, provided the operator has knowledge of the patient's condition. See 'The Chain of Life' by Dr. Guyon Richards, Health Science Press.

† See 'Interaction between Mind and Matter', Report of R. C. Firebrace and L. Landau, 'Light', March, 1957.

The question of *treatment* by such machines or methods is somewhat different. Psychometric or intuitive ability in choosing suitable remedies that 'fit' the condition of the patient, is probably often employed, under the name of a 'hunch', by the most reputable physicians, and unorthodox practitioners may, and often do, possess the same flair. But when it is claimed that radiations are sent out over many miles from a 'box', and the patient is said to have benefited, one must consider carefully the many and various elements that enter into the picture. It is only necessary to enumerate a few. There is expectancy, and the favourable suggestible state that results, which would itself promote healing no matter what method might be employed.* Then there is the unconscious healing power of the operator; it is quite possible that he may be a true healer in himself and in contact with invisible healing agencies. Under such conditions all the elements involved in psychic, mental and spiritual healing enter into the picture.

Where 'radiation rates' are set up on one or another type of radiaesthetic machine and are said to be sent out every so often to the patients, it seems probable that some sort of mental or emotional activity has been established which associates the operator and the patient through the machine, the latter acting merely as a link or key-factor.† Since it is claimed for such treatments that 'distance makes no difference', this in itself rules out any likelihood that the actual healing power is etheric or dense physical. Such a suggestion conflicts with all that is known of the laws governing the radiation of energy at the physical level. Indeed there is no known form of radiant energy that could be created by the mechanism used which could exert any appreciable influence at a distance of more than a few yards.

These criticisms do not imply that cures do not appear to take place in association with the use of these machines. What we wish to emphasize is that the diagnoses and treatments involved should be considered as psychic or extra-sensory phenomena, and that the claims made as to their being based upon purely physical science and its known laws cannot be substantiated.

---

* It is a recognized fact that fashionable medicines work most effectively for the first two or three years, when their efficiency begins to wane—thus demonstrating the high degree of suggestibility to be found in the average patient or medical attendant.

† A term used in modern parapsychology for the object or element that links the operator and the subject.

'SPIRIT' HEALING

The spiritualistic movement nowadays makes a great feature of its healing work. This is often referred to as 'spiritual' healing; but this is really a misnomer and should in no wise be confused with spiritual healing in the true sense of the word. In spiritualistic healing the so-called 'spirits', who are supposed to be directing the work, are considered to be discarnate human beings, and the term 'spirit' is applied to them without regard to any difference between spirit and soul in the human constitution.

Stated briefly, what is said to happen in spiritualistic healing is that a medium acts as the agent of an invisible healer, who works through him. Thus the actual healer is said to be the 'guide' of the medium, and is thought to make the diagnosis and either to prescribe, or actually to give, the necessary treatment. These 'guides' are described as people interested in healing, acting in the world in which they find themselves after death and not infrequently claiming to be distinguished doctors or surgeons who have passed over, or else 'medicine men' of Indian tribes or older civilizations. In the latter case the fact is overlooked that 'medicine' among such tribes or civilizations is in no way synonymous with what is signified by that term to the westerner of the present day.

Sometimes it is the medium alone who is consulted by a sitter; but more often it is a group or circle of people who 'sit' for the purpose of receiving advice and instruction through the medium. Whatever the details, the process involves a number of factors, of which several, if not all, will be found at work in any group or associated with any single medium.

(1)   The medium has always a personal interest in healing. This may arise from a natural capacity to heal, or may represent a means of fostering his own self-importance. At times it develops as a result of earlier experience in nursing, physiotherapeutic work, or some similar occupation. Mediums of this class often possess powers of vital-magnetic healing, as well as the capacity to sense the conditions in the patients who come to them. Others claim to be totally ignorant of medicine and even of the very rudiments of anatomy and physiology. Nevertheless a large proportion of them have, at some time or other, been connected with medical work in some form, and will admit to having had an abiding interest in healing for many years.

(2) Many such mediums have some genuine diagnostic capacity of a psychic order, either latent or active. This makes them instinctively aware of the difference between conditions of health and disease in the patient and of the location of strong or weak points in the body.

There is a certain danger in this for the person whose psychic sensitivity is of a too receptive character, for such people are apt to take the condition of the patient into their own vital field. Consequently they readily become identified with the sick person, feel the latter's symptoms in themselves, and then describe these accurately, as it were from their own experience. From one point of view, this may be a very useful way of gaining insight into the patient's difficulties. But the worst of such sensitivity is that the medium may not know how to rid himself of the identification and its attendant symptoms, and so may even 'catch' the patient's disease. At best the method is apt to introduce stresses into the medium's own being which are not only harmful to him but are liable to distort his judgment. In order to be safe, his attitude should be the same positive, yet sympathetic, detachment that characterises a good doctor or nurse. If this can be achieved, the sensitive will find that he is still capable of making a diagnosis, and all the more clearly because he avoids the confusion caused by bringing irrelevant factors, such as the patient's mood, into the picture he sees, or senses.

(3) The nature of the so-called 'guides' is certainly open to question. They may usually be assumed to be projections, in dramatized form, of some part of the medium's own personality, and not in any way independent 'spirits', or discarnate persons.*

(4) There is rarely any corroboration from the ordinary medical angle either of the diagnosis or of the result of treatment of cases. This is one of the main causes for the cynical attitude of scientists and of the medical profession in general towards the whole subject, since the patients are said to be 'cured' of diseases which the medium alone has diagnosed and for which there is no clinical corroboration.†

Nothing that has been said should be taken as suggesting a deliberate attempt on the part of mediums either to deceive or

---

* See 'This World and That', Chapters 7, 8, 9; Payne and Bendit. Also 'Man's Latent Powers', Payne. Faber.

† See Appendix B on investigations of such cases.

even to act as good showmen. Most mediums are entirely sincere, although they may be profoundly influenced by wishful thinking. Moreover, they often achieve definitely beneficial, if somewhat transitory, results among their patients. This happens from a variety of causes which frequently reinforce each other. The patient who benefits is usually suggestible, while the medium 'under control' is full of self-confidence, any doubts as to his capacity being stifled, so that his personality acquires a powerful and sometimes almost hypnotic quality. Moreover, the medium is often a good magnetic healer who, by restoring the flow of vitality in the affected part, gives at least temporary relief. Thus, if he is allowed by the believing patient to move a stiff joint, this joint may remain flexible for a time afterwards from the very fact that it has been moved and the muscle spasm relieved. At other times the healer may set the vital circulation going again with permanent benefit to the patient.

(5) *It is important to emphasize that the ability to diagnose does not necessarily imply the ability to cure or even to prescribe treatment;* a fact often overlooked by both the diagnostician and the patient. To establish that there is, say, a cancer, whether this be done by ordinary clinical means or by clairvoyance, is quite another matter from being able to say that an operation will be successful. The latter point only an expert surgeon can determine, and even he with reservations. But if the psychic diagnostician, because perhaps of some prejudice of his temperament, were to prescribe (and this has actually happened) a homoeopathic potency made from the eye of a potato, as a cure for malignancy, it would lay the 'healer' open to the charge of having perhaps caused the death of a patient whom ordinary methods might have saved. Similarly, for a 'spirit healer' to treat an abscess on the neck merely by magnetic passes, when a simple incision would normally lead to cure, with only a small scar remaining, not only prolongs the illness, but is likely to result in disfigurement from ugly scarring when the abscess eventually does burst.

Thus while psychic diagnosis can be most valuable, it is only safe when used in connection with clinical experience and common sense treatment.

(6) A word is necessary concerning so-called psychic operations which are sometimes claimed to be performed by a 'guide'. Usually these take place in cases where the sitter believes himself

to be suffering from a tumour, a malignant growth, an inflamed appendix, or some other serious condition calling for surgical intervention. At the sitting, he is told that the offending part will be removed, and, indeed, for the time being at least, he often feels much better. Such people will sometimes claim that they actually felt something occurring inside them; but others will say that they were aware of nothing of this sort at the time, but felt that improvement took place subsequently.

Unfortunately there is virtually never any clinical evidence of the alleged trouble in the patient's body. On the other hand, the *idea* was rooted firmly in his mind—a common enough experience in medical practice. What has been removed, or more likely, suppressed, by the suggestions of the medium, is the *idea* of the existence of a diseased organ, and not actual physical tissue which has become pathological. It can safely be said that the appendix allegedly removed in this way would, at some later inspection, be found intact.

There are some extreme cases in which a diagnosis of physical disease is suggested by the medium to a completely unsuspecting sitter, after which a 'cure' is brought about of a condition for which the only evidence is the word of the medium who also achieves the 'cure'. Such diagnosis and treatment are, naturally, not to be taken seriously or as being in any way related to fact.

(7) On the positive side it is true that patients frequently benefit from common-sense advice given by 'spirit healers', which is rendered all the more acceptable because it is believed to originate from some exalted spiritual source. Thus, special diet, exercise, relaxation, fresh air, and simple remedies may be prescribed with a reassuring technique that can in many instances be most effective, and result in real therapeutic benefit.

(8) Groups of 'spirit healers' often work on lines closely resembling those used in mental and absent healing and fully discussed in the section dealing with this subject. The fact that the group has a spiritualistic orientation may tend to attract to its meetings discarnate human beings interested in healing work. Other groups not using a medium are also at times assisted by these so-called 'dead' people, but there is not the same definite appeal for their co-operation as in spiritualistic groups. All such groups generate power which, *under the right conditions,* can do good.

CHAPTER VIII

HEALING CENTRES AND RITUALS

We so often expect God to do for us what he can only do
through us.
'The Perennial Philosophy', *Aldous Huxley*

HEALING LOCALITIES AND CENTRES

IT is a very ancient tradition that certain localities are places
of healing. In many cases a spring or well exists which is the
focal point of the tradition. We hear of the Pool of Bethesda, of
the River Jordan, of Lourdes, Rapallo, the Virgin of the Angels
in Costa Rica, and of many others, some of them being very
minor springs such as the Doone Well in Donegal. Originally the
tradition may possibly have developed from the fact that the
water itself possessed certain dissolved minerals or radio-active
substances which impart curative properties. The enhanced reputation of such places often begins with a vision seen by a simple
person like Bernadette, the shepherdess of Lourdes. The vision is
frequently of a feminine figure, and in Christian lands is usually
that of the Virgin Mary.

Once the attention of local people has been drawn to the spot,
the idea of its being a place of special healing takes root and its
reputation spreads. Whether or not the original vision was true,
such is the power of suggestion that a tradition soon develops
which, as time passes, makes the place a genuine centre of unusual
healing power. This is because more and yet more thought and
feeling accumulate around the original small nucleus, ultimately
creating a powerful vortex of energy, animated by the idea that
here is a place where miracles can occur. This in itself is sufficient
to invoke non-visible forces which strengthen and enhance the
atmosphere already created by man.

The existence of sacred places where healing readily occurs is
frequently mentioned in religious literature, but little attempt has
been made to study all the factors involved. The remarkable
effect of some of the most famous places has been noted, the
highly charged atmosphere being evident even to the doubting

mind. But little attempt has been made to study all the factors involved in these famous centres of healing.

The principles on which healing takes place in such localities are complex. There is in such spots a welling up of the vital forces in nature. These can, and often do, flow strongly enough to cleanse the vital field as well as the personal consciousness of those who go there seeking help. Such cleansing and vitalizing of the bodies permits radical psychological readjustment, if such readjustment be at all possible at the stage the patient has reached.

Those who are familiar with the unseen activities of nature know that natural surroundings are always instinct with vital energy. This is personalized in folklore in terms of fairies, gnomes and local gods; and folklore is right to the extent that natural life expresses itself in and through entities of many grades. Where human thought is brought to bear on a beautiful or isolated place, this natural life tends to become more co-ordinated and shaped, filling the patterns laid down by the human mind. Thus there is a coincidence between man and nature, so that they become linked, and reinforce each other.

In the course of time the vortex of energy formed around such a healing locality by the combination of human thought and natural forces not only grows stronger but becomes firmly established, and can be so powerful that even insensitive people are impressed by it.

Those who go to these places as pilgrims do so with the desire to be cured, and it is now acknowledged that there are sometimes quite unexpected and scientifically 'impossible' results. At Lourdes, out of the millions who have been there, some hundreds of startling cures have been fully examined and recorded, while there are many other successes less spectacular and convincing. Where the trouble is functional—that is largely psychological— and the patients are suggestible, physical conditions may indeed be relieved, if only for the time. It is always possible that such cures have nothing to do with the nature of the specific centre where the healing occurred; any other propitious environment might at that moment and for that individual have worked just as well.

A different type of healing which is none the less genuine also occurs, the sufferer going away physically as sick as before, but with an inner change that is reflected in his attitude towards his illness and towards life in general. This in due time fosters improvement in the disease conditions, if only to a slight degree.

Against all this, on the positive side, one must set off the millions who go away from Lourdes, as from other healing centres, unaltered in any respect.

Apart from cures by suggestion or total failures, there are thus two main classes of genuine healing at such centres—the unexpected 'miracle' of full recovery, and a beneficent alteration of the interior consciousness. Such healing can, of course, take place anywhere, if the patient is inwardly ready for it.* But the conditions in a powerful centre appear more propitious for the occurrence of such changes because of the specialized atmosphere and its concentration in the locality.†

Dangers and safeguards Mass hysteria regarding so-called miraculous cures often leads to gross exaggeration of results and may also produce harmful nervous reactions after patients have left the centre. Over-confidence and misapprehensions as to the limitations of the forces concerned as well as failure to realize the full implications of real and lasting cure, may under these conditions lead to frustrated hopes and profound depression. Credulity on the part of patients may also lead to the exploitation of valid healing power in the interests either of commercialism or of dogmatic theology.

In some very primitive communities, such localities are used for magical purposes and forms of worship along animistic lines; these may even include blood sacrifice. The healing forces so invoked at times involve the death of a selected victim, animal or human, or possibly the devitalizing of a child or relative. Fortunately such unpleasant practices are dying out, even in primitive communities, but—though rare—they do persist.‡ On the other hand, commercial exploitation and sectarian opportunism, based on any unusual phenomena, are all too common.

In the type of place we have been studying, the healing quality of the atmosphere exists spontaneously, and is then enhanced and specially conditioned by human agency, on the one hand, and by

* See Chapter IX. Also 'The Living Touch', by D. Kerin.

† 'The Miracle of Lourdes', by Ruth Cranston. McGraw Hill, New York. Also 'A Journey to Lourdes', by A. Carel. Hamish Hamilton.

‡ See 'African Traditional Religion', by E. C. Parrinder. Hutchinson's University Library. Also 'Pygmies and Dream Giants', by Kilton Stewart. Gollancz.

angelic co-operation on the other. Each of these factors can be studied independently, as in the following sections, but the essential thing in any place of healing is the co-operation of seen and unseen agencies, of man and angel.

The action of healing energies which derive from devic or angelic influence will be better understood if it is remembered that the life and energy of such beings is never complicated by interior conflict: it is always simple and direct. Consequently the intensely charged conditions at healing centres, full of this simple and beneficent influence, greatly help the patient to harmonize and adapt himself to the truly healing forces that are there available.

It may clarify the above to list the factors operating at a healing centre. They include:

(1) Expectation on the part of *the patient*, ranging from mild anticipation to unshakable faith;

(2) Differing types of *natural vital force*, varying with the locality, the tradition, and the type of entity attracted;

(3) The degree and quality of *public interest* roused and the conviction evoked as to the effectiveness of the centre;

(4) *Sacramental observances*, and/or healing services held;

(5) The consequent interaction between *the angelic influences* invoked and present, those performing ceremonies or otherwise acting as links, and individual patients.

HEALING GROUPS AND SACRAMENTAL AIDS

There are many forms of healing groups. Some are spiritualistic and claim to work under the guidance of discarnate human 'guides'. Some—usually connected with a church—consist of those who believe simply in the efficacy of prayer, while there are others which are independent of any special belief apart from that of the creative power of directed thought. In all, the purpose is that of trying to help the sick.

It is evident that people will not join in such work unless they have some genuine interest in the matter. Hence the common intention brings individuals together into a unified group, and— as is usual—the power generated is greater than the sum of the effort of the individuals present. But the keynote sounded, and hence the efficacy of the contribution made, will depend upon the aggregate quality of the thought and feeling of the members.

A group may, for instance, consist of somewhat woolly-minded people, deeply emotional or sentimental, yet devoted. The atmosphere will then be warm and embracing, but lack clarity and sense of direction. On the other hand, where the minds of the members are clear, they may tend to be too critical and analytical. Assuming that a group entity can be formed under these conditions, the atmosphere is likely to be cold and inhibiting.

What is required is clear but open thinking, coupled with emotional warmth that is without sentimentality. Balance is achieved by impersonality, both as to oneself and as to the cases under consideration, and by a sense of the manifold nature of true healing.

Every group must have a leader. Here again important principles are involved. The leader who dominates his group, either by sheer force of personality, or because he feels himself to be a chosen vehicle, tends to draw the vital and mental-emotional energies of the group to himself, and to direct them into his own preconceived mould. Such leaders are often people with an unconscious sense of personal power and importance, although consciously they may believe that they are wholly dedicated to the special service of Christ, or of some far lesser guide.

Groups led by such strong personalities nevertheless often achieve good results. A fanatic is one who concentrates energy through the very narrowness of his outlook, and gives it force in much the same way that water, flowing through the narrow nozzle of a hose, acquires an intensity it does not possess when flowing through a wider channel. Hence spectacular and immediate results may be obtained, but often they are not permanent. Yet if—as at Lourdes or elsewhere—the patient is inwardly ready, the impact of a strong current of fresh energy may release from within himself the genuine healing process.

The best leader is a person who has an innate sense of therapy, and who is aware that personal power and self-importance are dangerous. He sees himself merely as a channel through which impersonal healing forces flow, and his function, that of acting as a focus for the group as a whole. A good leader will have also an inner sense of the personnel of his group, and will impersonally select individuals with differing qualities who naturally fuse into a psychically balanced pattern. A group of this type develops a stable yet potent vital field, through which thought and feeling flow smoothly, and readily form a suitable medium for the inflow of spiritual power that is the basis of all sound healing.

Rituals. Many groups use some ritual in connection with their work. This may be in the form of simple prayer or directed meditation, or it may follow an ancient sacramental tradition. The value of such joint action is to help to weld the individual members into a group entity. People arrive individually and feeling separate, but if the meditation proceeds successfully, the consciousness of each member merges with that of all the others and creates a common psychic field, able to contain the healing energy that is later distributed to the patients concerned.

In the simpler rituals used in healing work, there is usually an offering of the group as a unit, a lifting up of the consciousness in thought or prayer or adoration to the Godhead; then a period of communion devoted to the healing of those who have asked for help; and a final distribution of healing power to all in need. This outline may be kept quite simple, or be considerably elaborated, but it is essentially present in all forms of group work. The object is to provide a channel of thought and aspiration that will be open to, attract, and distribute the healing forces of nature and of the invisible helpers and agents who are ever seeking opportunities for conveying healing and blessing to mankind.

If the ritual form is hallowed by antiquity and rests on a powerful tradition, this facilitates the gathering together of the many requisite forms of energy. If, in addition, the group is led by a consecrated priest of Christian or of other denomination, the inner link which gives him power to administer sacraments is a further factor in focussing and energizing the collective psychic field.

To be effective as a leader of a group a layman must have a real sense of dedication to his work. A priest brings with him a certain impersonal authority and power, derived from his office, which acts automatically as a channel between the visible and the invisible worlds. If the personal dedication and the priestly function are combined, the work is greatly enhanced. But a priest who has no sense of the reality of healing and who performs his office perfunctorily, may—in this matter at least—be less efficient than a truly dedicated layman. For the efficacy of any healing group depends upon the ability of those present to invoke, and to channel without distortion, the specific agencies which can act for the purpose of healing the sick. How exactly this is done, whether by priest or layman, whether in an ancient shrine or a room in a modern house, is a secondary consideration. A combination of intelligent thinking with a strong tradition and sacramental power, in a place dedicated to the work, provides the best possible conditions.

Ritual forms vary from the use of diverse rites and the administration of consecrated elements of some sort—such as the bread and wine of the communion service, or the reserved Host, or sacramental oils, with at times elaborate ceremonies of purification preceding the administration—to the mere gathering of a group of people who sit in silence, willing to be used for healing purposes. Purification beforehand is usual in the primitive rites of healing. The Hawaiian medicine men, for instance, insist on a full confession of sins previously committed before any healing rite can take place. The healer then cleanses the body with long passes of his hands, and throws away the 'evil' so extracted into fire, or into a bowl of water that is then cast into a river or the sea. He may then recharge the patient with healing energies. A ritual form that works well usually has these same elements in it: confession, purification, and a renewing of life through a sacrament or other religious act.

The results of the group method of healing are difficult to estimate. Often the patients are receiving other treatment, which may or may not be beneficial. Although many patients declare that they have been profoundly helped by psychic or spiritual influences no serious investigation has ever been made: the treatment and the needs of the patients are too hard to assess. Moreover, although groups meet and consider individual needs with a view to restoring the patients to health, there is usually no insistence upon a particular result. There is a subtle distinction between suggesting and demanding results. Ample testimony certainly exists that many patients have gained comfort and peace from the ministrations of a group, and such a change of attitude may make a return to health easier, or it may ease the transition to the life after death. It has been said many times already in this book that individual healing takes many forms, from complete restoration to health to release from the physical body, and that any of these forms may be valid for the person concerned.*

---

* This subject has been treated in 'Meditation', by Adelaide Gardner, Chapter VIII. Theosophical Publishing House, London.

SUMMARY

From all that has been described in this section, it is clear that while the forms employed may vary, the essential elements in healing group work remain the same. These may now be summarized.

(1) The *patient* in need of help;

(2) A *group of healers* who meet together with the intention of assisting the patient to recover;

(3) A sacramental, or other, *formula*—often very ancient;

(4) The *forces invoked* by the leader and his group, with or without ritual aids. Some questionable primitive rituals invoke earth, water, or fire elementals, which can be very unpleasant, but may be efficacious for the simple people concerned.

So far as has been noted by the students compiling this study, the form used is of less significance than the purity of heart, the dedication, the sincerity, and the harmony of the members of a group. Quite simple, unlettered people, meeting with an earnest desire to help others, and living a purified life in order to 'be worthy' of the privilege of helping, can make a powerful and effective interior vortex for healing purposes which the unseen forces will, and do, undoubtedly use.

HEALING ANGELS

The word *angel*, as used in Christian writings, means messenger, and implies the function of bearing messages or commands from God to man. The Hindu term *deva*, literally 'shining one' or 'illumined one', can be held to include the function of conveying knowledge or wisdom from a higher to a more material sphere. In Gnostic and Kabalistic literature the teachings about angels is very considerable, certain groups of angels being associated with various elements in nature, or with special activities. Among these Raphael, a mighty Being, and his cohorts of attending servers, are recognized as ministers of healing.

From the viewpoint of this book, angels or devas are recognized as agents for the concentration and distribution of psycho-spiritual energies. They are considered to be intelligent beings of a non-human order of nature that runs parallel to the human kingdom. They work unseen in the subtle, and hence invisible worlds. Angelic activity consists largely in carrying out the laws of nature, without questioning their purpose or validity. It is an old axiom that while man may question, angels automatically, and with complete satisfaction, obey the One Will.*

Angelic workers are of every grade of intelligence, some far more evolved than ordinary men, and having as their work the guarding of certain forces in nature, even of great cosmic influences. Others are of minor capacity, carrying out tasks under direction from their superiors.

The densest types of these unseen workers are the nature spirits, sometimes seen as shining centres of light, and sometimes assuming the forms built for them by human thought—when they become comic or elegant or fantastic according to the tradition of the area, their actual work in nature, or the mind of those observing them.

Other groups work with subtler matter, and appear to clairvoyants as flashing streams of colour, associated with ritual, music, crowd activities, strong feeling and all forms of natural growth.

Individuality is not the chief characteristic of the angel or devic kingdom. Only the higher orders of angels have individuality and power of choice comparable with that of human beings. Those in the highest ranks are immensely potent, and have charge of an extending hierarchy of the lesser orders. In healing work, the group associated with such activities is, as we have said, under a lofty Seraph traditionally called the Archangel Raphael. Rank on rank of workers receive the influences poured out through him, and distribute these, as opportunity arises, throughout the whole world.

The human mind can give clear and useful direction to these healing forces supplied by angelic workers. Such co-operation is intended, and healing work gives a great opportunity for its expression.†

* Christian writers frequently place the Angelic Hosts as a higher order of evolution than man. Other and older traditions see the human and the angelic streams of evolution as running parallel to each other.

† Those who seek to know more about the subject of the angels and nature workers may read 'Fairies at Work and Play', by G. Hodson; 'The Kingdom of the Gods', G. Hodson, and 'Fairies', by E. L. Gardner. The last gives evidence for their existence. Theosophical Publishing House, London.

Thus in the work of psycho-spiritual healing there are—as we have noted before—two immediate sources of energy. The one is human, and generated directly by the human mind. The other is non-human in its source, and may come from any level of the unseen world around us, from the most earthy to the highest spiritual sphere.*

Healing groups, or individual healers, are likely to be in close, even if unconscious, touch with some non-human entity in the invisible worlds. It does not follow that such an entity is necessarily of a very high order. It may be, and often is, of a somewhat primitive and elemental nature, which is able to convey powerful but undifferentiated energy, derived from one of the "elements"— earth, air, fire or water. It is surprising how potent such energies can be, and hence how forcefully they augment the strength of the group or person to whom they become attached. At the other end of the scale of possible unseen helpers, there may be a glowing Being of great power and range, whose radiant life is of the spiritual rather than the psychic order, and to whom the term angel is certainly applicable.

When such entities are perceived by a human being, they are almost inevitably clothed in a form to which the observer is accustomed. There are many reasons for this, some of which are explained in the literature on the subject. If one expects an angel to be radiant, winged, clothed in long white robes and possibly crowned, that is the form in which he will appear. If the observer has derived his thought image from descriptions in which the angels of Raphael are said to be mauve and green, with shimmering lights, he will see precisely this. Such images are subjective, created by the human mind, and may be ensouled by any entity who is at that moment present. True interior perception, unconditioned by preconceptions, shows the members of the angelic hierarchy to be swiftly moving vortices of specialized energy, focussed around a centre of intelligence. Their radiance varies with their tonal quality, their nature, and their work, but it cannot be truly represented by any known physical colours.

The exact function of angel helpers in relation to healing groups and to individual healers is difficult to define. As far as has been observed, they appear to overshadow and enhance the healing atmosphere. The group aura is, as we have said, a vessel into

* Obviously both elements draw on the ultimate power of the One Life.

which psycho-spiritual energies can be poured. The human members contribute their quota and the angelic helpers bring with them a further supply of healing life from their own interior sources.

The presiding angel is the executant of the group, and gathers up and distributes available energies according to the directions given by the human leader of the group. Thus as each institution or ill person is named, a suitable measure of healing energy is directed to that person or place. The angel appears to act as a filter, so that no patient will receive more than he is able to take. Thus a patient may be highly receptive, or insensitive, or even inaccessible to help from the inner worlds—yet in each case the presiding angel adapts the available life-force and sends whatever is possible and appropriate to each patient.

It is usual to speak of an angel helper in the singular, but this is an oversimplification. The angelic kingdom is, as we have noted above, essentially hierarchical in organization, and a single superior Being is served by an infinite number of subordinates who appear to be on call at any moment, and who automatically fulfil the intent of their superiors.

The keynote of the best type of co-operation between man and the angel kingdom depends, so far as human consciousness is concerned, upon holding the mind clear and open at the higher mental levels, those which register abstract truth and idealistic concepts. This, from the human viewpoint, means—once more—deep impersonality, a detached, though very kindly, point of view. In healing work, compassion and the will to help will obviously also be present. The human being thus brings all within his power to contribute, and his collaboration with an angel helper may be roughly expressed as: 'Do with this what you can, and what—in your wisdom—seems best'.

CHAPTER IX

THE PRACTICE OF SELF-HEALING

For behold, the Kingdom of God is within you.
Luke XVII, 21

IT should by now be abundantly clear that—in the strictest sense—all healing is self-healing. Medicines may alter the balance of metabolism, or modify the nervous activity; psychologists may help a patient to release himself from deeply buried conflicts or fixations; magnetic treatment may loosen a block in the flow of vital energy; but unless the patient himself *permits* the benefit to continue, picks up the improved situation, and continues to keep the healthy activity moving, there will be no permanent cure, but a return to the same trouble or the development of a new one in its place.

It has also been pointed out that—consciously or unconsciously —it is often the patient who defeats the attempt on the part of others to cure him, and that the attitude of opposition to cure is generally deeply unconscious. Outwardly A wants to get well and urges the doctor to help him, yet nothing gives relief. B goes to doctor and healer to be cured, but remains an invalid and unable to earn his living. C exercises, diets, studies health magazines, yet remains asthmatic and undernourished. The will to be well is conscious, on the surface. Below there lie roots of retreat from life, the need to be looked after by others, or a sense of interior conflict which prevents the healthy flow of psychic and hence of physical energy. It is when some external treatment coincides with an interior adjustment that 'miracles' occur, and the patient—with a fresh view of his relation to life—throws the self-interested habits of invalidism overboard and becomes a contributive member of society.

It follows that the practice of self-healing demands of oneself the capacity to keep on seeing life anew, and so to draw on deeper and richer stores of energy from within oneself, rather than from without. Helps may be used—such as intelligent dieting, exercises to keep the spine and muscles flexible, good breathing habits and the like, and specific medical treatments. But the essence of self-healing is the recognition that within each one of us there lies an infinite source of power, peace and psychic vitality, upon which each can draw for the legitimate purpose of work, and service to others.

It is evident that for sustained self-healing, the building up and maintenance of active health against the odds of, say—a second or third rate constitution, the strain of earning a livelihood in a congested district, and life with uncongenial companions—there must be a fairly continual practice of communication with the higher levels of one's own consciousness. This may be unconscious, as in the self-forgetfulness of a devoted parent who draws entirely unconsciously on the divine Life, because selflessness is one of the ways of its expression; or again through an intense devotion to duty—as when doctors and nurses plough through a period of epidemic, constantly overworking under pressure of events and physically exhausted, but without collapse. Or it may be through the regular practice of some form of silent contemplation, a deliberate turning of the personal life to that of the Infinite. There are many other possibilities, but one way or another, the channel between the personal bodies and the life of the Self—so abundant, so perennially *there* for our taking—is being kept open and used.

In the history of sainthood, as of modern students of psychology, periods of 'dryness' or failure are recurrent happenings, and much that is known about them applies to the problem of self-healing. Things go well for a while, and then comes a check. Energy flags, tempers get scratchy, the light in the world—and from within—seems darkened. In modern psychological parlance there is need for a 'fresh objectivization' of the situation. We do not see ourselves truly in relation to life, as it is at that moment. Some element of self-will or self-repudiation has crept in, of subtle hatred or withdrawal, of self-interest or self-pity, and we do not see the intruder for what it is. Therefore it poisons the psyche subtly, insidiously, until some physical symptom betrays us to ourselves.

A student is fortunate, if at such moments, there is a congenial or more experienced fellow-worker with whom frank impersonal discussion is possible. A patient may be able to get help from his physician or psychologist. Failing this, a clue often comes from a book, a chance-heard phrase, a dream that shows up clearly the root of the present block in the flow of life. 'I thought I was being so *nice* to that troublesome new worker, but I suddenly saw that I was downright jealous of his popularity'. Or one imagines that long forgotten wrongs have really been assimilated, and suddenly an old weakness reveals itself in new guise: 'My old trouble! I always *did* want to meddle in other people's affairs!' or 'I have always shirked responsibility and now I'm doing it again!'

Then comes an act of self-reorientation, a loosening of hold on the past and on the personal, a letting go of the grip that justifies itself because of this or that—so important at that moment. Quietly—like a rootlet seeking water—the innermost turns to the *One,* lets go all hold on the intricate interwoven pattern of personal behaviour, and in utter simplicity is washed clean, refreshed, renewed, in the immensity and the peace of the Inner Life.

The compulsive person, driven by fear, habits of conformity, or unsatisfied desire, often displays demoniacal energy. Never ceasing from talk or action, such people may work for years at express speed, and even die suddenly in full activity, or drop into invalidism when the nervous system finally collapses. The self-healer touches a fount of life of far richer power, for its origin is his own Daemon, the Angel of Light within, which draws its vigour from the illimitable Source of all, and sustains effort with gentle strength. This latter Source is truly without limits, but it needs the discernment born of the habitually quiet mind to use its power with sagacity.

KARMA AND HEALTH

THERE is a familiar Christian saying, 'Whatsoever a man soweth, that shall he also reap'. The law of cause and effect in science states the same fact. E. W. Sinnott, in 'Mind, Matter and Man', recently published in the World Perspective Series, extends the causal idea further. He writes: 'Pain has a necessary value, for like the white strip painted along the middle of the highway, it warns us when we stray from the right course. ... If we are free to choose our course, we must expect to suffer if the course is wrong'. In Hindu philosophy this causal relationship is called the law of karma.

Such a principle, if true, is highly relevant to health, disease and cure, as to all other aspects of life. If it were understood, it might supply the explanation of accidents and illnesses that are not easily cured, as well as why, after years of searching for a cure, one is suddenly found—sometimes even through a 'wrong' method, from which no result could reasonably be expected, and which has no medical justification. Moreover this idea can help an intelligent patient towards the mental attitude that will be most conducive to cure, or if that is out of the question, to finding happiness despite some grave disability.

The fundamental principle of the law of karma is that man is, at any given moment, under the influence of forces which are derived from causes that he has himself set in motion by his own acts, whether these be mental or physical, 'good' or 'bad'. These forces reach him from the past, although this is far from obvious in many cases. It is clear enough that the effects of setting fire to gunpowder, or the social punishment for a crime, are direct expressions of the law of cause and effect. But when a person is afflicted with the results of bad physical heredity, such as a disease which cramps his whole life, or suffers from an accident apparently due to another person's negligence, or to natural cataclysms, the sequence is not so easy to discern.

The doctrine of karma presents no scientifically verifiable proof, but this is held to be due to the shortness of man's memory, limited as this is to events in any one life, recorded in and through the physical brain. Yet if some part of man is, as is assumed, immortal, the field of unconscious memory can be taken to extend much further through time than does the memory of the purely physical consciousness. If there is a central part of man, always continuing from one phase of existence to the next, it would form a permanent focus for the action and reaction of such forces. Such phases of existence are held by those who uphold this law to be a series of incarnations in the physical world, recurring cyclically. A cyclic systole and diastole is seen everywhere in nature, so why not in man?

Briefly, the theory of karma is that every individual comes to birth with a certain load of unresolved forces, both constructive and destructive, at work in himself and in his relationship to his environment. Past acts, past attitudes of mind, are the root of these. And if a man has had much experience through many lives, the accumulation of such forces may be very considerable. This 'load' has to be worked out, and more or less consciously coped with, at some time before he reaches his ultimate goal—which is variously called salvation, liberation, *nirvana*, *moksha*, or the like. His debts have to be paid, he has to collect whatever debts are due to him from others. But, more deeply, he has to learn to integrate whatever such physical and psychological relationships mean to him, so that the experience they denote becomes part of his spiritual and eternal heritage.

The study of this doctrine in depth is a vast one, and out of place in an appendix of this kind. But its application to the problem of health is of prime importance, for it implies that the individual, and he alone, is responsible for what happens to him. It is he who evokes his parents, bringing him good or bad heredity, good or bad living conditions; and as life goes on, it is he who evokes the illnesses and accidents that beset him, as well as all the pleasant things which he enjoys. To some extent this is the view of modern psychology, that if we are ill it is because something in us wills us to be so. And this 'something' is the law of karma, seeking to restore a balance disturbed by ourselves, and now reacting on ourselves.

This may seem cold comfort to the sick person. And indeed if it results on his part in the passive attitude of 'It's my karma, I can do nothing about it', or on the part of others in anything savouring of callous indifference, it makes of the world a very harsh environment, even if it be a just and equitable one. But karma should not be seen as an inevitable fate about which nothing can be done. A situation may arise which derives from the far past of the individual, but there are also more recent factors which play upon it; more important still, there is the fact that what happens at the present moment introduces new forces which become causal to the future. One is generating karma *now* just as one has generated it in the past. One's immediate actions and one's mental attitudes towards the situation in which one is, in short, alter the overall picture of past karmic forces at every moment of time.

Karma is thus a dynamic balance, not a book-keeping transaction resulting in a credit or an overdraft on the bank of Life. As such, every factor in the environment, including the reaction of the inner individual to this environment, has to be considered in the total karmic pattern of the moment. And that pattern alters all the time, as the balance of forces changes.

A doctor, nurse, or healer, or any other person contacting a sick person, is thus part of the karma of that individual. In this sense there need never be any fear that one is 'interfering with karma' by giving what help one can. If one had not a contribution to make to the situation—for better or for worse—one would not be there. Thus if a sick person, after years of suffering, meets the 'right' doctor, that is the karmic moment for him to receive effective help. But in just the same way, the fact that a patient has for so long had the 'wrong' treatment, or no treatment, or been unable to benefit from treatment given, was because the balance of karmic forces—including his own attitudes—was such that he was tied down to his pattern of illness. It is only when some change occurred in this balance that the new factor, the right doctor, *could* enter the picture effectively.

The balance of karmic forces is thus both subtle and intricate, and not a matter that can usually be clearly worked out. The important thing to realize is, first, that whatever difficulties occur, they are self-created; and equally, that only the self which created them can—in the long run—deal with them effectively. Moreover, in the ambit of every individual there is an active process of sifting and canalizing the total of karmic forces, so that he is never faced with more than he can actually bear. He may indeed be strained to the uttermost, but he is nevertheless intrinsically able to take the suffering involved if he so decides, without breaking down utterly under it. The total sum of unbalanced karmic forces in the case of undeveloped individuals could easily be too much to be dealt with at any one phase of life, i.e. in any one incarnation, were it not for a merciful selection (held in the Hindu philosophy to be in the hands of certain spiritual Intelligences called the Lipika) the individual might easily be overwhelmed and swept under.

Thus in the case of illness—and for that matter in happy experiences also—the individual who accepts the idea of karma can ask himself, 'What am I doing to deserve this?' and if he is in pain, 'What is there in me that perpetuates this misery? In what way is my attitude towards it, or towards life itself, in error?' And if this leads him to learn the lesson he has to learn, he may find himself quickly and unaccountably free of that situation.

MEDICAL AND RELIGIOUS COMMENTS ON THE RESULTS OF SPIRITUAL HEALING

IT has been pointed out in the text of this book that it is impossible to accept unequivocally the claims made by various types of spiritual healers. The reason is twofold; the lack of supporting evidence, and the confusion which exists as between spiritual and psychic or paranormal methods of healing. The word spiritual is too often used loosely and with no evidence that the source of healing power is other than the enhanced personality of the operater, and while it is true that the writers believe paranormal or psychic healing methods *can* be effective, they find it difficult to substantiate that belief in terms of case material. The same is true of other scientific investigators who have made sincere investigations into this subject.

It is of little use for the so-called spiritual healers to argue that such scepticism as is solely due to prejudice, though prejudice may be present. The medical profession, like every other body of human beings, does not like to have its traditional views upset. But there is just as much prejudice on the part of most would-be healers against having their own theories and beliefs investigated. Thus the whole subject falls between two opposing points of view which are based, not on reason and scientific considerations, but on antagonistic concepts and strong feeling.

There is also the question of discrimination as to what it is worth while for the scientist to investigate. Olaf Stapledon used the phrase 'intrinsic improbability' with regard to certain subjects he had not thought it worth while to study, because a *prima facie* case for them had not, to his mind, been established. When reports are circulated of miraculous cures which seem extremely improbable to one who knows anything about the nature of the animal body, it takes something more than unsupported assertions to arouse interest among the scientifically minded, let alone to persuade them that it is worth the effort and the expenditure of energy to follow them up. This does not mean that scientists have not gone into the matter; indeed members of the medical profession, in collaboration with the churches, have done a great deal in the effort to arrive at definite conclusions—but have, so far, failed to do so. This was also the view of the late Canon Anson, who was himself very much concerned in investigating similar material. He told some of the writers that he had never seen a *conclusive* result due to psychic or spiritualistic healing alone. And this is the experience of many.

The most objective assessment so far comes from Dr Louis Rose, in an article in *The British Medical Journal* (Dec. 4, 1954). His paper is worth quoting, as it represents a serious attempt to study the results in about a hundred cases, mostly taken from a 'spiritual' healer who has, through the press, a vast reputation, yet whose books are completely lacking in objectivity and give no evidence for the results claimed. Dr Rose went about his enquiry in a proper way, and his analysis of ninety-five cases may be summed up as follows:

(1) In fifty-eight cases it was not possible to obtain medical or other records, so that these claims remain unconfirmed.

(2) In twenty-two cases the records were so much at variance with the claims that it was considered useless to continue the investigation further.

In this group a case is quoted where a woman was discharged from hospital as incurable, and had to wear a surgical belt for thirteen years. The healer cured her, but not of any physical disease which could be checked from her medical records—in other words, the trouble was probably hysterical and the cure was by suggestion. Another case reported in the press as a wonderful cure had no benefit from the healer *until two years afterwards*, when she felt relief—but herself attributed it to the treatment she had been receiving in a clinic at a hospital.

(3) In two cases the evidence in the medical records suggests that the healer may have contributed to amelioration of an organic condition.

(4) In one case demonstrable organic disability was relieved or cured after intervention of the healer.

These statements show that Dr Rose's mind was not closed against accepting the possibility of cure being brought about by the healer.

(5) Four cases showed improvement but relapsed.

(6) Four cases showed a satisfactory degree of improvement in function, but no change in the organic state of the tissues.

(7) In four cases there was improvement when healing was received, *but the patient was also being treated by orthodox medicine.*

(8) One case examined before and after treatment continued to deteriorate.

This report shows the difficulty of finding out just what has happened to the large majority of cases. It is fairly certain that, had proper clinical evidence been forthcoming, a larger proportion of cases helped might have been found, while on the other hand, other claimed cures would probably be found to be invalid. The same difficulty as regards evidence besets any other investigator, whether it be of spiritualistic healers, sacramental healers, or radiesthetic practitioners. It is rarely that one of these is willing to allow even a modicum of independent investigation. Yet this is essential if the true facts about paranormal methods of healing are to be properly assessed.

One cannot help concluding, therefore, that the miracles widely advertised in the sensational press are for the most part highly dubious and open to more mundane explanation. Yet real miracles do occasionally occur, unobtrusively and usually without publicity. Indeed, it may even be that the very fact of seeking to achieve spectacular cures would tend to inhibit the occurrence of true healing at any depth below the surface, or in cases other than those amenable to suggestion.

This, in effect, was the substance of the conclusion arrived at by the *ad hoc* Committee of the British Medical Association set up at the request of the Archbishops' Commission on Divine Healing in 1954, and summarized in Section 29 of their report as follows:

'... as there are multiple factors—whether of body or mind—which may contribute to the precipitation of an illness, so there are multiple factors which conduce to the restoration of health. Since man is a unity and health a condition of full functioning, we cannot afford, especially in critical illnesses, to disregard any means at our disposal which may lead to the restoration of a man's health, since all the functions of the personality react upon one another. The emotional life of an individual has a direct bearing upon his physical well-being as everyone knows who has experienced what it is to be depressed and to be happy. Religious ministration on whatever basis it rests may have an important bearing upon the emotional and spiritual life of the patient and so contribute to recovery.'*

This Committee, dealing with the healing brought about by religious ministration, thus concluded that no clear case can be made for this type of healing *alone*. The writers of this book, while agreeing for the most part with this conclusion, nevertheless recognize that occasionally an apparent miracle does take place brought about by paranormal agencies, but that this can only occur when the increased ability of the patient to readjust himself, at different levels of consciousness, makes it possible for the deeper and hidden resources of Life to flow through him.

* See 'Divine Healing and Co-operation between Doctors and Clergy' Brttish Medical Association, London, 1956.

SHORT READING LIST

GENERAL

Alexis Carrell: *Man the Unknown*. Hamish Hamilton.
Erich Fromm: *The Art of Loving*. Allen and Unwin.
Raynor C. Johnson: *Nurslings of Immortality*. Hodder and Stoughton.
C. G. Jung: *The Undiscovered Self*.   Routledge, Kegan Paul.
Kenneth Walker: *Patients and Doctors*. Penguin Books Ltd.

THE HEALING PROCESS

M. Beddow Bayly: *Basic Principles of Health and Disease*.
                                    St. Clements Press, W.C.2.
Arthur Guirdham: *A Theory of Disease*. Allen and Unwin.
Arthur Guirdham: *Disease and the Social System*. Allen and Unwin.
D. Kerin: *The Living Touch*. Bell.
A. Newsholme: *Health, Disease and Integration*. Allen and Unwin.
Leslie Weatherhead: *Psychology, Religion and Healing*.
                                    Hodder and Stoughton.

PSYCHOSOMATIC MEDICINE

Groddeck: *The Unknown Self*. C. W. Daniel (out of print).
Stephen Barton Hall: *Psychological Aspects of Clinical Medicine*.
                                    H. K. Lewis.
Max Hamilton: *Psychosomatics*. Chapman Hall.
Desmond O'Neill: *A Psychosomatic Approach to Medicine*.
                            Pitman Medical Publishing Co., London.

SPECIAL STUDIES

P. D. Payne and
   L. J. Bendit: *This World and That*. Faber.
Abbé Mermet: *Principles and Practice of Radiesthesia*. Vincent Stuart.
Divine Healing and Co-operation between Doctors and Clergy.
                            British Medical Association, London.

THE ANCIENT TEACHINGS

A. Besant: *The Ancient Wisdom*.
                            Theosophical Publishing House, London.
H. P. Blavatsky: *The Secret Doctrine*.
                            Theosophical Publishing House, London.
Hugh I'Anson Fausset: *The Flame and the Light*. Abelard-Schumann.
A. Gardner: *Introductory Studies in Theosophy*.
                            Theosophical Publishing House, London.
Aldous Huxley: *The Perrenial Philosophy*. Chatto and Windus.
Kenneth Walker: *So Great a Mystery*. Jonathan Cape.

INDEX

QUEST BOOKS
are published by
The Theosophical Society in America,
a branch of a world organization
dedicated to the promotion of brotherhood and
the encouragement of the study of religion,
philosophy, and science, to the end that man may
better understand himself and his place in
the universe. The Society stands for complete
freedom of individual search and belief.
In the Theosophical Classics Series
well-known occult works are made
available in popular editions.